T0121999

The Passionate Long Walk to the Awakening of a New Life

KATHERINE STEELE

BALBOA.
PRESS

A DIVISION OF HAY HOUSE

Balboa Press books may be ordered through booksellers or by contacting:

Balboa Press
A Division of Hay House
1663 Liberty Drive
Bloomington, IN 47403
www.balboapress.com.au
1 (877) 407-4847

Because of the dynamic nature of the Internet, any web addresses or links contained in this book may have changed since publication and may no longer be valid. The views expressed in this work are solely those of the author and do not necessarily reflect the views of the publisher, and the publisher hereby disclaims any responsibility for them.

The author of this book does not dispense medical advice or prescribe the use of any technique as a form of treatment for physical, emotional, or medical problems without the advice of a physician, either directly or indirectly. The intent of the author is only to offer information of a general nature to help you in your quest for emotional and spiritual well-being. In the event you use any of the information in this book for yourself, which is your constitutional right, the author and the publisher assume no responsibility for your actions.

Any people depicted in stock imagery provided by Thinkstock are models, and such images are being used for illustrative purposes only.
Certain stock imagery © Thinkstock.

Print information available on the last page.

ISBN: 978-1-4525-3003-1 (sc)
ISBN: 978-1-4525-3004-8 (e)

Balboa Press rev. date: 02/27/2018

Contents

Acknowledgements

My thanks to my dear friend Tessa Fraser, my first genuine real friend, for her acceptance and wonderful ability to listen; to Betty Williams for her wisdom, her friendship, and being a mother figure in my life; to Robert and Lorraine Wilson for their generosity and for providing me with a sanctuary when I needed it; and to Andrew and Ella Hodges for their patience, encouragement, and belief that this book would finally come to pass.

I'd also like to express my gratitude for my wonderful family: my eldest daughter, Kate, a smart, compassionate woman with the ability to communicate on all levels; Lourdes, my second daughter, who brings us the gift of humour and remembering birthdays, and the lesson of pushing through life, especially when times are tough; my son, Jeffrey, with his wonderful sense of humour and loving insightfulness into all situations; Rachel, my youngest daughter, whose independent nature has driven her to succeed, and whose dedication to connecting to her roots and heritage is wonderful; and Geovani, my best son-in-law—my only son-in-law—whose generosity has made this book happen. To all of you, thank you for the unconditional love you have poured out onto me.

CHAPTER 1

The End of Life as I Knew It

It was the summer of 1973. The days were long and hot, and I was reading the book *The Song of Bernadette*. I loved the story of how Berndette Soubirous met Our Lady in a grotto and was given messages that were to eventually spread all over the world. All this had special meaning to me. I was expecting my second baby, and if I had a girl, I planned to name her Lourdes, which is the little town where the apparitions occurred.

The day arrived, and I delivered my little girl, Lourdes. She was so beautiful with her dark hair and peaches-and-cream complexion. But my joy quickly turned to sorrow. Like my first daughter, Lourdes was born with a cleft palate. This time, however, it was much worse. She had no roof to her mouth, and I could see into her nasal passages. I knew she would be difficult to feed, with no palate to give suction on a bottle. Not wanting to hear any more bad news, I tossed aside suggestions from the nurses that there were even more problems than this.

Before leaving hospital, I spoke with a mother who had just had her third baby. We first met one afternoon when she had just arrived, and I didn't see her again until a few days later. Quite a few of us new mothers had gathered out on the balcony one afternoon to chat. I had just said, "I think I will cry a few tears over my baby" when I turned and noticed one mother still in her room. I walked over to her and spoke to her, thinking perhaps she was too shy to join the others. We seemed to hit it off straight away, and as she was leaving the next day, we said we would stay in touch—and we did.

At home, I was surprised to find how truly difficult the feeding process was. I became irritated. Each feed dragged on for an hour, slowly, ever so slowly. Because her suction was very poor, I had to put my finger under her chin and moved it up and down to help her drink the milk. Two hours later, I would repeat the process all over again. It soon became obvious I was up against some big hurdles. Thankfully, John took over the night feeds, patiently feeding her and trying to get her wind up. There were sores on her back where the constant rubbing and patting irritated the skin.

To make matters worse, the feeding bottle was very small, and the process of stretching the teat over the bottle often ended in a mess, with the bottle skittering across the table. When the milk spilt everywhere, I cried in frustration.

Milk poured out of my baby's nose as I tried to feed her, so I had to tilt her head far enough back that I knew that the milk was going down her throat. I despaired of being able to help her. Green mucus from an infection appeared at one point, pouring from her nose and out onto her pillow. My days became a battle of trying to keep her going while also caring for my two-and-a-half-year-old, looking after my husband, and maintaining our home. My emotions soon plummeted into depression. The darkest time in my life was upon me, and I was ill-equipped to cope.

I had been raised in a home where a lot of conflict was the norm, and this left me with anxiety and not a lot of confidence in myself. As a young person living at home, I had a job as a secretary and I worked hard at it. The job filled my days, but returning home every evening with no one to talk to left a huge gap in my life. My mother didn't want conversation, and neither did the rest of the family. It was as if we were strangers, each going about our day yet all living in the same house. Sometimes to get attention, I would cause an argument—just to feel as if someone *cared*.

The one quality I possessed was an ability to stand up for myself. I hated being taken advantage of. My stepfather and I often fought, and on one occasion, I was pushed up against a wall with my stepfather's hands around my throat because he was angry I wasn't helping with the weekly wash downstairs. That only reinforced my belief that he was an intruder who made our lives miserable.

Of course, in hindsight, I know that he lived with post-traumatic stress syndrome, and that caused a lot of the conflict in our home. As a soldier fighting the Japanese on the Kokoda track, he had seen too much for his soul to bear. But none of this was understood at the time. Knowing what I know now, I have a huge feeling of gratitude for what he did for us. I appreciate his efforts, in spite of his problems, to go to work every day, pay the rent, put food on the table, and pay for my college education.

One Sunday after Mass, a prayerful lady from our church noticed I was crying. She came over to me and asked what was wrong. I poured out my heart to her about my baby daughter's predicament. Her immediate response was, "I will send away for a relic of St. Bernadette, and when it comes, just pin it to her clothing." When the relic came, it was the tiniest piece of fabric placed on a round disc, encased with a plastic covering. The edge was stitched in blue.

When Our Lady of Lourdes appeared to Bernadette Soubirous, she wore a sash of blue around her waist. She asked Bernadette to go to the water. Bernadette started to dig in the ground; she got mud on her face, but eventually, a spring came forth with blessed water. Now pilgrims from all over the world come to this blessed place for healing. Where once there was just a grotto, a cathedral now stands.

All of this meant a lot to me as I pinned the relic to my baby's clothing. Sometimes it ended up in the wash, as I forgot to take it off. I do believe now, as I did then, that there is a power taking care of us, in spite of all that goes wrong in our lives. If I had the faith of a mustard seed, maybe I could have seen through all the tragedy and been more peaceful about my lot in life. But as each day brought fresh trials, my faith often wavered.

There is nothing that brings a mother down quicker than a crying baby. Her nerves get frazzled, and her confidence flies out the window. The dream of a perfect baby slips away, and all that is left is a hollow heart and tears. I watched the other mothers leave the hospital with their babies who fed and slept peacefully. Why was I in this battle for life? It would have been easier to just let her slip away, but I couldn't do that; I had been entrusted with her life.

Many times I phoned my friend Tessa, who I met in hospital. In deep despair, I poured out my troubles, and she listened. She never flinched or turned away. My interactions with other people were different. I asked my mother-in-law to babysit Lourdes for an hour or so one morning while I took care of some business. When I returned, I found she hadn't bothered to change the baby's dirty nappy. There was quite a mess. I asked why, and it was very clear she couldn't cope with a baby who had problems. I never asked her to babysit again.

As my friendship with Tessa grew, we started to visit each other. She lived out of town, about a half-hour's drive into the country. The first time I drove out there, I got lost. As I am not good with directions, I felt like giving up. Instead, I drove back down the dusty road and found the property. The house was quite a distance from the road, so over the cattle grid and in through the fields I went. She came out of the house and down the stairs, and she greeted me with a warm smile. A day spent together, talking, drinking tea, and having lunch was a balm to my spirit. When I returned home in the afternoon, I felt refreshed.

Those visits to my friend were a godsend, and I will always treasure how she treated me with such respect. I knew she was a very shy person. When Tessa told me that after her mother had died when she was just twelve years old, she had been asked to take care of the family of six, even though she wasn't the eldest, I understood. It was a big ask, but she stepped up to the task, and this is where her strength came from.

CHAPTER 2

Tragedy in Hospital

Sitting at the table one afternoon, I thought in despair, *How am I ever going to go on?* Suddenly it came to me: I had to make a pact to survive. The doctor who had delivered Lourdes had just died from cancer, and as I had known him a long time and respected him, it was to him I gave my allegiance. Later I would change it to myself, but for now, he was my rock to build on.

I looked to women who were strong. Lady Cilento, a doctor and also a mother who had written books on how best to raise children, became my mentor. Even though I had never met or spoken to her, her words upheld what I was trying to achieve. My eldest daughter, Kate, flourished in spite of all that was going on in our household. Headstrong and confident, she fetched and carried to help me. She was a real light in those dark days. Blonde with long curly ringlets on either side of her head, she was the exact opposite of her sister. Lourdes was silent and had dark corkscrew curls, while Kate bounced along and was a social butterfly.

During this painful time, no one came to my door to ask if I needed help. It was like a conspiracy of silence – stay away, they've got troubles. Surely someone cared! But no one came. It was up to me to move forward, step by step, and face whatever arose – even cruel criticism by those who neither cared nor understood what it was like to have a child with a disability. Judging another person because of looks or behaviour brings out the worst in people. I believe their deepest fears come to the surface, and they feel it is their right to attack in this way. I have learned to let it go, like water off a duck's back. Back then, however, it was just more pain. The learning curve I was on was huge, and fear gripped me like a vice.

I looked up one afternoon as I was feeding Lourdes and saw a black cloud twisting and writhing around the door close to me. I felt if it came near, I would die. I didn't want to look. Next thing I knew it was on me and seemed to swallow me up. A statue of Venus de Milo I had on the stereogram suddenly turned grotesque. I thought I had lost my mind. My grief was profound, and no one understood how I felt.

At my mother's urging, I joined a little group of women who were learning to weave at our local TAFE school to temporarily take my mind off my troubles. The group was large, and I noticed that the teacher often bypassed me to work with others who she thought would be more successful with their work. As with any new venture, the group soon dwindled to just two of us. Weaving is a painstaking process. She asked me to stay as she would lose her income if I left. So I stayed on, making some progress on the mat I was making on a bicycle frame.

Out shopping one day at the local plaza, I ran into my teacher, and before I could utter a word, she said, "What's wrong now?" Her words struck me like a blow to my heart. She wasn't interested in me at all—she only cared about having me in the class to save her income. Going home that afternoon, I reflected on what had happened. I realized I had been copying my mother's behaviour, going out with a sad look on my face, hoping someone would care. I learned a very powerful lesson that day. Never again would I go out showing my pain. People just don't want to know. They are caught up in their own troubles, big or small.

From then on, when the makeup went on, so did the smile. I sometimes think back to that occasion and thank that lady for the lesson, even though it was painful at the time. It has stood me in good stead over the years. Sadness doesn't bring friends. A smile and a kind word have a greater effect in the long run.

As we were new to the neighbourhood, I had hoped to make some friends with those I met in my street. We had been away for several years, travelling around Australia in our caravan, so when I fell pregnant we bought our first home and settled in. John was a hard worker and took his work life seriously. He was meticulous about turning up on time, and accepting out of town work, which others didn't want to do. Which meant he would drive late into the night to get home on weekends, often being on the road up to six hours. This went on for several years. Of course, this sacrifice of family time did bring its rewards, his wage included a lot of overtime, which helped considerably with the family income. We took a lot of pride in the house and garden, and weekends were spent concreting under the house, building fences and garden beds, and renovating our home to make it our castle. I have always been a gardener, so I planted beautiful roses along the front fence. People would stop and admire them.

Our home was within walking distance of our local church, which we attended regularly, but it takes time to get to know people, and we were still the new kids on the block. I was introduced to some of the ladies from the church and hoped to reach out and make friends. One lady seemed open to friendship, saying, "If you feel like getting out of the house, just come round for a cuppa."

I was having panic spasms, so I decided to walk the short distance for the visit. With the baby in the pram and Kate walking beside me, we set off. Upon reaching her house, I could hear this lady on the phone with a friend repeating something I had told her in confidence. I didn't even bother to knock, I just turned round and went home. I would need to look elsewhere for friendship.

Mornings were especially difficult. I felt as though I had horses' hooves pressing on my chest. I didn't want to get up and face another day. My husband paced up and down, as I was making him late for work. I felt guilty that I wasn't a better mother.

We were advised by the baby clinic to buy a special milk formula to fatten Lourdes up for her surgery, which usually was done twelve months after birth. I don't remember the name of it anymore, but this formula was three times more expensive than the normal brand most mothers buy, and it was also recommended for hole-in-the-heart babies who faced surgery. It was difficult to make up and had to be just the right temperature. If the water was too cold or too hot, it didn't work, and that batch had to be thrown out. I would make the bottles up at night for the next day, and I soon learned how to do it correctly. I approached the company that produced the formula and asked if they would sell it to me by the carton and maybe at a reduced price, I never heard back from them.

My days were filled with a baby to feed, an older child to take care of, my husband, and the house. I was tied to the house, and my only day out was to go shopping with my mother on a Thursday. My focus was on getting my baby strong enough to face surgery. I decided I had better get my driver's licence, as it would be easier to drive into town than waiting to catch a bus, juggling two small children and all of the extras needed for a day out. I sat the written test with a migraine headache and then went right on to the driving test and passed it straight away.

The date was set for surgery to have Lourdes's cleft palate repaired. We drove to the city, a ten-hour trip, and booked into an old accommodation house in the heart of the city. The room was sparse, and heating baby's bottle involved a long walk to a bathroom down the other end of a long corridor. There was no running water in the room. It was very primitive, but it was all we could afford.

The surgery was to be performed by a plastic surgeon, as the operation was quite complicated. Flaps of skin taken from inside her nose would be brought across to make a bridge for the roof of her mouth. Our first child's operation was done by a surgeon who described it as "like taking off a toenail." But to young parents entering this phase of handing your child over and trusting all will be well, it is scary. Placing faith in the doctor and the hospital to see this episode through brings with it a real wrenching of the heart.

We took our curly-headed baby to the hospital. It was on a hill, and finding a car park wasn't easy. Our nerves were frayed and our tempers were short. We took Lourdes in and got her settled, and then we were asked to leave. Parents weren't encouraged to hang around and wait.

We came back a few hours later to find the doors to her room locked, and upon enquiry we were told to just wait. My heart was pounding, and I was thinking the worst. It seemed like an eternity before we were allowed into the room to find our baby turned upside down on oxygen. No one spoke or even looked at us. We asked, "What happened?"

The answer was brief. "She had a clot lodged in her windpipe after surgery, and she was dead for four minutes."

I was dumbfounded. "How could this happen? Why wasn't someone watching her?"

Once again, we were asked to leave. We stumbled out of the hospital, and I just cried and cried in deep despair.

It seemed like life was lurching from one disaster to another. I don't remember a lot about the rest of that day, only that my heart was broken for my beautiful baby. Coming back to the hospital the next morning, we found her with cardboard cylinders on her arms to stop her from putting her hand to her mouth and damaging her surgery. The nurses were force-feeding her, and it was a terrible sight. My questions were met with stony-faced silence or a clipped reply. It wasn't much different when I asked the same questions of the doctor in his surgery after Lourdes came out of hospital.

They all knew what had happened, but no one wanted to talk about it. Does no one understand the hearts of parents when faced with such tragedy?

CHAPTER 3

Taking One Step at a Time

We came home from the hospital, and life became even more difficult. I found that my baby could no longer drink from a bottle; whatever she had learned in the first year of her life was wiped out. Getting fluid into her had to be done with a spoon. Around this time, I started to make up a cereal to help her with her everyday meals. Little did I know, I would go on making that cereal for another three years. It was all she would eat.

The baby clinic where I would sometimes go to get her weighed was of little help. One visit was a turning point into even more sorrow. "I think your baby has autism" were the words I heard. I didn't know what that was, nor did I want to know. It sounded like a death knell. Everywhere I turned, people either made statements about my baby's condition or looked blank.

Lourdes was sitting in her high chair, and a nurse had come to check on her progress. Her little face was contorted with screaming. The nurse just gave up and walked out. I didn't see her again. I was back to being alone. I drove down to see one of my mother's friends one day, who was a nurse, hoping to gain some comfort from her. She looked at Lourdes, sitting in the back seat, and said, "I don't think she has mental retardation, her eyes are too bright." It was the first glimmer of hope.

My days moved forward ever so slowly. By now, infection was a constant part of my daughter's existence, so she was given antibiotics, up to fifteen times a day. I sat on the floor with my baby and felt my life was not worth living. I can still see the spot on the kitchen floor where I sat, with my back against the cupboards, in such deep grief that my life had come to this.

Then it came to me: *If I can just get through the next hour, then I might be all right.* An hour passed, and indeed, I had survived. I made it my focus to just make it through one hour at a time, even if all I did was to give her another dose of medicine and just sit there. I was living an exceptionally difficult life and I knew it, so I took the flashlight off the major problem and shone it on small chunks of time. That was all I was capable of. I had control over my life that way—one hour at a time. It was like the ocean. It was too big, so I surfed one wave at a time.

I chose not to see a doctor about my depression. That might seem strange now, but I had seen what happened to someone I knew, and it was horrible. She had depression after giving birth to her second child, and for some reason she didn't respond to treatment with tablets. She was then given electric shock treatment, and it wiped out all of her good memories and only left the bad ones. To counteract that situation, she was given stronger and stronger medication. I had seen her on one occasion, standing at her kitchen sink whilst her knees convulsed of their own accord. It was shocking to watch. I saw how many times she would go through her day in a robotic trance, and it frightened me.

The fear that I could be like that was too much, so I stayed away from doctors. To help myself, I followed the teachings of Dr. Claire Weekes in her book *Self Help for Your Nerves*, and it steadied me and helped me believe I could recover. I rang her at her home in Sydney and spoke to her about my life. She said, "You have a lot of courage."

That surprised me. "How do you know that?" I asked.

"Because of the way you are talking," she answered. She also said that "all of this is making you very sad," and I agreed with her, but now I felt I had an ally in the world, a very powerful one at that. She was known for her work around the world in curing people who had suffered a nervous breakdown, and I felt that, just by speaking and listening to her, I would be cured also. The cure eventually came; it took a long time, but I did it on my own terms.

CHAPTER 4

A New Baby

T he year 1975 was another pivotal one in my life. My third child was born, just two years after Lourdes. I had been sick for the whole nine months, and during the pregnancy was ordered on bed rest in hospital, as I was bleeding. Late one afternoon, a beautiful old nun came past and stopped to enquire how I was doing. I poured out my heart to her, and her words were like a balm to my heart. "Don't think about problems," she said. "Just be confident of a perfect child."

Indeed, Jeffrey arrived healthy, the heaviest of my babies at seven pounds two ounces. But I wasn't ready to carry the load. A nurse was sent up to see me and talk to me about her life having a son with mental retardation. She was very kind in many ways and even offered to dress Jeffrey in his special clothes for the trip home. I was grateful for the support. Whenever I came across someone who seemed to carry a heavier burden than myself, it gave me hope and the courage to go on.

This beautiful son was the easiest of my babies. He rarely cried, was patient until I could get to feed him, and seemed to be sent to show me the joy of living again. He just fitted in with our life, which was now busier than ever.

One hot day, my mother came over for a visit. She had been urging me to take Lourdes to a paediatrician for some time now to get some help. We were talking in the kitchen, and I looked out the window and was amazed. Lourdes was sitting on the lawn, and the hose was trickling water. She was dipping her fingers into the water and licking them. That was a turning point. I had to find more answers and move on.

I asked my mother to come with me on the paediatrician's appointment to give me courage. She sat out in the waiting room, and I walked into the lion's den. This man was renowned for being blunt, and I copped it in spades. He asked questions about her birth and progress. As we stood up, my little one lay on the floor and started screaming. He said, "Of course you know, she will never amount to much. She may be able to count money and do menial tasks, but that's it."

I stumbled out of the room and repeated what the doctor had told me. My mother just looked at me with sadness. My heart plummeted in deep despair at his words. It was a shock. I had gone looking for answers and came away with a mountain of sorrow. The way he delivered such words to a young mother so bluntly, without compassion or mercy, has stayed with me. I can only forgive him his lack of understanding and wisdom shown to me in my darkest hours.

The deep pain and sorrow were reflected around our house. I was glad when my husband asked me to drive him to work each morning, as he was working on a big project. His company was building a library at the university. It was raining, dull and overcast, but the little break in the routine was welcome. My husband had been made leading hand on the electrical side of the job, and he was feeling out of his depth. Both of our lives were in the pits.

My mother could see how upset I was and suggested I join a writer's club to give me something besides sorrow to focus on. She was right, God bless her. It is strange how events unfold. Just after I joined, the editor of the writing group wanted to step down for a while, and she thought I should take the job. Feeling in over my head and not very confident, I decided that maybe, with some help, I could give it a go.

Previously, the group's little magazine had been edited and printed by our local university, which seemed to take forever. Now I thought, *I've got the skills to type and print it myself,* so I took a vote of the members. Only one was against the idea, so now I was editor and publisher. I jumped in with both feet, often staying up till two in the morning to get the job done. The energy seemed to come from nowhere, and I had something positive to focus on.

I kept the position for three years and then stepped down. That experience gave me the confidence to build on, and in the years ahead, I went on to bigger and better projects.

CHAPTER 5

❧❧❧❧

The Beginning of Learning

My darling child was now four years of age and well into a world of her own; nothing seemed to penetrate that darkness. The screaming sessions whilst out shopping (although I took sweets to try to distract her) were unbearable. Other shoppers just stood and stared or made comments about that horrible child. When we were having lunch at a shopping centre one day, my little one dipped her hand into a glass of lemonade and licked her fingers, and a man who was sitting nearby commented in a very loud voice, "Take that pig out of here." I had to pretend not to notice, but it hurt.

At home, it was no better. We had bought a rocking horse and put it out on the front patio to encourage her to ride it and get some relief from whatever was tormenting her. It was no use. She would stand next to me and say, "Is it going to rain today?" over and over again. Repeating, repeating, repeating. It drove me insane.

I was out shopping with my mother one day. I can still see where the shop was and how it happened. It was so strange. A voice suddenly said, "Go into that shop." It was a bookstore. I went in and thought to myself, "What now?" The voice said, "Look up," so I looked up and there on the top shelf was a reading programme. I bought it and walked out of the store.

That program, even though it was hard work, was a blessing. It distracted both of us from our sorrow, and we worked every day. It had large cards with words on; I would show Lourdes the card, tell her the word, and get her to repeat it. To my amazement, she repeated the words, and her memory became stronger. Even though progress was slow, something was happening. We did the reading three times a day for a year, never relenting, no matter how tired we both were. Little did I realize, I was instilling into my child a love for reading, which has paid off big time. Her reading and writing skills are just wonderful. Whenever she visits me now, she picks up a magazine or book, and I marvel at the sight.

In addition to the reading programme, I knew I needed to get her into a kindergarten, which would help with socialization skills. I chose one at random, and oh what good luck awaited me there. Upon hearing my story, the lady who owned the kindergarten said to me, "I can help you. This is do-able." What music to my ears. She was a motherly type of woman, and obviously my daughter would be in good hands.

The first few months were difficult, as Lourdes didn't want me to leave and would cling to my legs as I tried to get away. It was like prying an oyster out of its shell. Little by little, she found her place, and for me to have some time to myself was a godsend. She loved painting pictures, and I have a large black and white photo of her, brush in hand, looking contented. There is an old Chinese saying: "The flower that blooms in adversity is the rarest and most beautiful one of all." She was that flower.

At the end of the year, there was a fancy dress parade to give the children a chance to show off. I dressed Lourdes as a little Dutch girl with a pink top, black vest, coloured skirt, big hat, and clog shoes made of white cardboard. Pigtails were plaited and pinned inside the hat. Kate went as a queen of hearts in a beautiful blue satin dress with a big cut-out red heart pinned to the front. They both looked gorgeous. Out of around thirty children, Lourdes came in first. I was so thrilled.

None of these experiences, though, seemed to give her the enjoyment that would have shown on another child's face. It bothered me. Photos of her showed a child looking down or with a serious expression—never smiling. There was a sadness about her, like some sort of cloak that she wore.

Her night-time behaviour just haunted me. After I put her to bed, she would sleep for a couple of hours and then she would start a long wailing sound. It was eerie. All I could do was go in and comfort her. This went on for several months.

She couldn't bear the sounds of fireworks. Her ears were so sensitive, it took years before we could go and watch the display at the show. We would sit in the car some distance away with the windows up and marvel at the sight of the coloured lights.

She had a condition called *glue ear* and required grommets to be inserted to drain the inner ear. Sometimes they lasted a year, sometimes not. We were constantly taking trips to the ear, nose, and throat specialist to have this condition taken care of.

By the end of Lourdes's fourth year, I wondered, "Can she go to school?" I approached a friend of mine who had a large family and was also a teacher and asked her advice. She said, "Go over to the school" which was adjacent to her home and "talk to a teacher." I did, but when I explained my situation, they didn't seem very interested. I was told to enrol my child at the office.

I sewed uniforms for Lourdes and got everything ready for the big day, not knowing if this was the right thing to do. *What if all this is for nothing, what will I do now?* kept going through my head. As I watched her from the front door walking up the street with all the other kids to catch the school bus, I cringed and thought, *Good Lord, her school bag is half her size.* What on earth was I thinking? I didn't back down, though; I wanted to know, was she capable of learning in a school environment?

Wouldn't you know it, she scored a teacher who certainly didn't understand how to handle her and put her desk outside the classroom with her in it. I couldn't complain; I was already skating on thin ice. I wanted to give her a chance at life—the best. I could have sent her to the special school for children who had limited capacities to learn, but as her behaviour was so bad, I felt she would just copy the others. In mainstream schooling, I was hoping normal behaviour would show her a better way.

I subscribed to a monthly magazine, and one day I saw a book advertised about a woman in America who taught emotionally disturbed children. I just knew I would find an answer in it, so sent for a copy. There I found the words, "Ignore the bad and praise the good." I repeated these words to myself over and over like a mantra. How was I going to apply this?

Little by little, I got going, looking for some speck of good behaviour to praise. There sure was an awful lot to ignore. The battle my child was going through was within, and I didn't know what it was all about, other than an enormous amount of pain.

Children who have cleft palates need to have speech therapy—and lots of it—to get their speech to a level where it sounds normal and doesn't have a nasally sound. The palate needs to be trained by repetitive sounds. After surgery, the next step is daily work to bring this about. The speech therapist was very kind and patient, and her little book with all the lessons in it was carried to and fro with each visit.

One day, as the therapist and I were talking, I asked, "Do you think my daughter is retarded?"

She thought for a moment and said, "No. I think she is too independent."

We visited the plastic surgeon who had done the operation, and he commented on how hard I was working and how much the speech therapy was making a difference. I nearly fell off my chair. He was not a man given to praise. I came outside into the sunshine and felt good. We were making progress.

Speech therapy requires years of work to take effect, and it has to be worked into everyday life. Later would come elocution, which is the next step up in refining speech and added another several years to her program. I was often tired beyond belief, but I was on a mission to help my child. Looking back now, I wonder why I was so driven. Perhaps it is just my nature, but I do remember as a child always wanting something better. Because we had so little, I vowed one day to have a beautiful home. Maybe my dreams were bigger than me.

Grade two now showed there were more problems. It was like peeling an onion, layer by layer. Eye/hand coordination was added to the list. A combination swing and slide with a big ladder to climb up to strengthen her muscles, was built by John, so that each morning she could go out into the garden and swing to her heart's content. A trampoline and a large ball for rolling over, needed to be purchased, and exercises done every day. Crawling on the floor, going through tunnels, and training the brain were things that had to be done every day. We needed glasses to help her eyesight … the list was endless. I approached the government and asked if some financial help could come our way. Sorry, they said, but your child doesn't qualify. In other words, she had come so far that she was no longer in the category which defined whether help was forthcoming or not. I just laughed. I was saving the government money by helping my child. This was a lonely road to be on—no recognition, just trudging along with no end in sight.

CHAPTER 6

The Early School Years

Grades three and four for Lourdes were more settled, as she had a teacher who had compassion and understanding. Neither of us knew the diagnosis—that was to come much later—but for now, she was a little kid in school, trying to fit in with the others. She was small for her age, and in the school photos she was always placed in the front row. Sometimes she had been so ill with ear infections that, when the photo was taken, she turned away, looking very sad. But then, she never made eye contact with any of us either. That had to be taught. "Look at me when you want to tell me something, Lourdes," was a constant refrain.

It wasn't easy to fit in at home either. She was always the odd man out. With the time that I poured into her doctor's visits, surgeries, speech therapy, and so on, it seemed to the others as though she was the favourite child. Not so; she just needed this support if she was going to have any kind of a normal life. Coming home one lunchtime after I had just dropped Lourdes at school after speech therapy, a neighbour asked me why was I bothering with all of that. She had a child with a cleft palate, and it was very obvious by his speech—which was nasal and muffled—that he wasn't getting the attention he needed.

Kate had made friends in the street. We lived in a cul-de-sac, and with about a dozen houses and around twenty-five children, there was no shortage of someone to play with. There was often a game of cricket out in the middle of road, and when the cars came and went, they just shifted the rubbish bin—which was the wicket—out of the way, and then returned and went on with the game. Kids flitted from house to house, often squabbling amongst themselves. There were more girls than boys. Often one house was the favourite to play at, and then another. Kate had her favourite playmates, and her life progressed along a normal path. Her childhood memories are positive, and as the eldest child in the family, she has a special place in our hearts.

She also had a talent for music, so we bought an old piano, and music lessons started. The teacher was a crotchety old guy, and although he was trying to instil a love of piano in my child, sometimes the lesson ended in tears. I didn't think that was the best way to learn. So I changed teachers, and to this day, that second teacher has nothing but praise for Kate's talent—even though, at times, my daughter would not read the music and play by ear. Dire threats were certainly made along the way that "if you don't practice, I'm pulling you out of music." It worked like a charm eventually. She found her niche and went on to play the organ at church and team up with a friend in the neighbourhood to sing together for weddings.

Music is still a big part of Kate's life. Even with four children of her own, she still finds time to play at church on Sunday. She started her own business teaching very young children the importance of making music. As time permits, she plays some evenings at pubs and clubs. She is a high school teacher, and her life is extremely busy.

Jeffrey was a quiet child, often sitting in the lounge with his Legos spread all over the floor. He had a friend from up the road who would come and play. We had a sandpit under the back stairs, and the pair of them would sit for hours, often not talking, playing make believe with their toy cars. It was strange. His friend often stayed all day to play, yet not once did he eat at our place.

At school, Jeffrey fitted in easily, and his report cards showed him to be an average student. His friend was playing soccer, so we enrolled him in a Saturday game, which I often sat and watched. One Saturday morning, I went to my mother's house to have a cup of tea and chat and lost track of time. By the time I hastily drove back, Jeffrey was nowhere to be seen. I drove around the area looking for him—and then a motorbike pulled up with Jeffrey on the back. I was relieved and scared at the same time.

I gave him a dressing down about getting involved with strangers. It must have made a big impact, because he no longer would go shopping with the girls for gifts at the shopping centre. After that, he went to the corner store and did his shopping. Poor little guy; my overprotectiveness probably made the whole situation worse.

His primary school years were easy, and home life for him went along much the same as always. With grades nine and ten, he seemed to be lost in the mix, so I decided to send him to a boarding school. Fortunately, the principal was a young man who had the gift of remembering each boy's name, and he greeted each one on the playground with, "Hello, how are you today?" and then he said that boy's name. I was impressed, as remembering names is not my strong point. With hundreds of boys at the school, that took considerable effort.

Right from the start, it became obvious that Jeffrey was having a difficult time fitting in. I drove down to the school and, after talking with the counsellor, said to him, "Look, son, there are plenty of kids here to make friends with. It's like picking fruit off a tree. Just choose some." With three other young guys in his dormitory, I couldn't see the problem. As his confidence grew, so did his friendships, and today he has many friends, born out of his early experiences at boarding school. I am so proud of him.

Years eleven and twelve were still difficult for Jeffrey, and at times he begged me to let him come home. I knew that if he hid himself away at a local school, there wouldn't be much progress, so I insisted that he stay. He was learning to come out of his shell, and today he has very pleasing social graces. His easy laugh and thoughtfulness are beautiful gifts and have eased my heart in troubled times. The way he looks deep into a situation and the words he speaks are pure magic. Maybe his life hasn't panned out exactly as he would have wanted, but as a young man with sincere qualities, I am sure he will go a long way when he finds his niche in life. He has a beautiful singing voice and sang at Kate and Geovani's wedding. He has formed a band and plays guitar and sings at pubs and clubs. His job, even though full-time, still gives him time to play around with his music.

Lourdes success in her primary school years depended upon the type of teacher she happened to have. I don't recall the teachers from grade five to grade eight, but what I do remember is going to the school at the end of each year and seeing Kate's and Jeffrey's teachers first, leaving Lourdes' teacher for last, as I knew the assessment of her work would be disheartening. Lourdes excelled at English—her reading and writing were great—but maths was hopeless. I hired a retired schoolteacher to help her with maths after school. Trying to keep up with what was being taught in the class was too difficult for her.

Many times, I questioned whether I was on the right path, trying to stay the course to give her an education which would help her in years to come. I knew the other subjects were not so important; if she could grasp maths and english, she would be able to read the newspaper, sign documents, read books, handle her own money, and hopefully one day get a job. It was a far cry from the prognosis given to me all those years ago. I didn't set out to prove the doctor wrong, even though his diagnosis stung me. I wanted to know what hidden potential was under that mantle.

I had read stories of people with brain damage relearning after suffering major trauma. Maybe there was a miracle waiting for Lourdes also. It was often one step forward and two steps back, trying to instil an education on all fronts, not just school but socialization, good behaviour (I often failed on that one), and just generally getting along in the world. Was I pushing too hard? Yes. But the genie was out of the bottle, and I couldn't put the cork back.

CHAPTER 7

❆❧❆

My Friendship with Erich Krell

*O*ver the years, I had been sent a bundle of Christmas cards from a group whose members painted by foot or mouth, as the artist had lost the use of their hands. The cards were copies of original paintings done by these artists. I marvelled at what a difficult task it would have been. I decided to write to the association and ask if there was anyone who would like to correspond with me. A month or so later, a letter arrived in the mail. It was from one of the painters, Erich Krell, who painted with a brush in his mouth.

He had been a German tourist here in Australia who used to play soccer and was involved in a car accident that left him as a quadriplegic, with no control over his body from the neck down. As a young man left in this condition, it must have been horrific to discover how much his life was never going to be the same. After about a dozen surgeries and rehabilitation, he was confined to a wheelchair. In our frequent letters to each other, he told me of the drugs he had to take so that he could sit up straight and to stop muscle spasms from catapulting him out of bed. Strapping him down was of no use; all it did was lacerate his body.

To meet this man, my family and I travelled to Adelaide, South Australia. This visit was a privilege that I am sure he did not extend to everyone. He was a very private man. I was amazed at how he managed to do his paintings, some of which were twenty-four by thirty-two inches in size. He could only manage to do them by painting half of the picture upside down. When we were there, he was painting a red cardinal bird, and he actually had a stuffed bird sent to him from a museum so that he could be precise in its authenticity. Attention to detail was everything to him. I asked him if he had come to terms with his life of being in a wheelchair, and he looked at me very directly and said, "*Never.*"

His battle to survive and to learn a new way of living was humbling. To prove that he could be part of the association took years of work—and then to be finally accepted meant he would have an ongoing income. For someone who played professional soccer to then have to sit with a brush in his mouth to earn his living must have been an enormous leap of faith. To go from being an energetic young man to being tied to a wheelchair … I can't imagine his pain. I know he had a temper; he was open about it in his letters, and sometimes he raged at the injustice of it all. He told me that, at one stage, he lay on the lounge room floor curled up and just wanting to die. He tried to will himself to death.

He had a carer who came and went, but the domiciliary care service only provided nine-to-five services five days a week—no night shift, no weekends, no holidays. He did manage to travel overseas, but the production that effort required must have been bigger than Ben Hur. Over the years, the only people he found who might have been able to help were a so-called Christian couple who wanted to sign a deal that they would help out but only if Erich's house and contents, his valuable works of art, and his stamp collection were handed over to them at the time of his death. They made it very clear that they were saving him from "rotting in an institution" What sort of people are they, who want to profit from someone else's misery?

I had the privilege of Erich's friendship for several years, and I always looked forward to his letters, often six pages long. I never took for granted the effort he had to put into his writing—a stick in his mouth, one keyboard stroke at a time.

His paintings were sold all over the world. I never asked the price, but with his meticulous attention to detail, he certainly was one of the most sought-after artists who painted with a brush in his mouth. His honesty about his life was, to me, a testament to a man who, faced with the most difficult of circumstances, looked life squarely in the eye and said, "I will be bigger than you." He has since passed on, but I will always remember his integrity and sheer grit. What a privilege!

CHAPTER 8

※<del></del>※

Support Group for Families of the Disabled

*T*he year 1980 was a major turning point. I had decided I wanted to find other people who were in the same position as myself—hopefully, another mother whose child had the same problems. I had joined a group that did horseback riding so that Lourdes could take advantage of this social activity. The gentle movement of the horse while she sat in the saddle would help stimulate her muscles, and it would also have a calming effect.

I asked around the group of mothers of children in the riding group, told them of my plans, and invited them to come. Several seemed interested, so that was a start. I printed out flyers, hundreds of them, and took them to several agencies that provided services to the disabled. One evening, a voice on the phone said, "I don't think much of your idea. I don't think it will work." That woman never joined, but the ones who did made it all worthwhile. There were more than thirty ladies at my first meeting.

I kept a logbook of the meetings and went around the room asking names, addresses, phone numbers, and the name and disability of each member's child. It seemed all of them were looking to me for something that was missing in their lives. I, in turn, was looking to them to find people I could talk to who would understand the mystery that was so tightly locked away: where the boundary for *normal* was and where the disability took over.

I held the meetings monthly. I included films that I thought would be of some assistance and books that I thought might help. I left the meetings open in attempt to discover what the members wanted, and I was often frustrated to find there were no forthcoming ideas. I wanted more for the group, and I ended up banging my head against a brick wall. A friend suggested that the answer was obvious: "All they want is a cup of tea and to whinge." I couldn't accept that. There had to be more to life than the status quo. I had a lot to learn about people and life. After recommending a book to one of the ladies who I thought could be helped by it, I was told, "I threw it in the corner, it was a load of rubbish."

I was invited to sit on a few committees with some of the principles of disability organizations. Eagerly I shared my ideas, only to find that the big guy got up each time and claimed the idea as his own. I soon learned not to be so eager.

A woman called me a number of times to talk to me about her disabled son. I urged her to come to the meetings, but she seemed unwilling. One day, a bit fed up, I said, "Oh well, it's up to you," and left it at that. She was there at the next meeting. This was a woman older than myself by about twenty years, and little did I know what a godsend she would prove to be. Looking back, I feel she was sussing me out, to see if I was fair dinkum about what I was doing. I felt empowered, and yet at the same time it was like I was spinning my wheels, going nowhere. Most of the women in the group were supported by agencies who had programs set up for their children. I had to set up my own programs.

My new friend loved shopping and asked what I was wearing to the conference coming up. My answer of "I don't know" was soon met with a shopping trip to buy clothes. I was never keen to do that—any time I wanted to get something new, I just bought the item and came home. None of that sashaying around the shops for hours; it just bored me. But this time, off to the shops we went, with Betty choosing skirts, tops, dresses, all flung over the screen, with a constant haranguing of "try this on, try that on" and me whipping the clothes on and off and making quick decisions, yes, no. What a way to shop! I'd had never had an experience like it.

The naming of 1981 as the International Year of the Disabled was a turning point. It led to a lot of ideas coming forward to be heard. I was asked to be a representative for my city and attend the conference in Brisbane. Over the course of three days, I saw disability in all of its forms. At times I was shocked, watching crippled adults dragging themselves across the floor, or a mother who had two children with Down's syndrome. There were 150 of us parents from around the state who had come together, and it was time to shake up the status quo.

Doctors, who had held sway for too long, acted like demigods in people's lives, as if they knew all the answers, when in fact they didn't. The gate had been opened, and a flood of ideas poured forth. A lot of people really didn't understand about their rights and had been kept in the dark. A new manuscript was now being written, with guidelines about those rights. That didn't mean everything was going to be all right all of a sudden. It did mean that disabled people now had a voice, and it was up to them or their carers to put those ideas forward and not take a backward step.

Fear would be replaced by power. That was what I had been fighting for all along. I think my German ancestry of stubbornness and my Irish fighting spirit had risen up in me, and now there was going to be change. I could smell it in the air.

There were panels to discuss health issues, education, and the rights of the disabled and their parents. My question of "What about my rights when my child is in hospital and disaster strikes? Who is answerable to me?" was met with blank stares.

The doctors were clearly out of their depth to guide and advise the parents, who themselves were floundering in their lack of understanding of their rights and services. We wanted more for our children than just put them in care, walk away, and forget. The battle lines were drawn, and there was no going back. Onwards and upwards we pushed, even though no path was visible at the time. We carved our own paths in the wilderness and stood proud of the journey. I know I did. I was excited by the other parents' determination to succeed, which in turn fired my imagination to do more and have more.

My friendship with Betty blossomed. As it turned out, we had similar backgrounds with our families: parents who weren't really there for us a lot of the time and having to take a leading role in our own marriages. It was an uncanny mix. With more experience in life, she also became in a way my mother and my sister as well as my friend. I had gone looking to find answers for my daughter, and I found a friendship that lasted thirty-two years.

Betty's son was severely disabled, with cerebral palsy and intellectual disability and her day-to-day life with him was a much bigger challenge than what I was facing. Some of the most common signs of intellectual disability are: rolling over, sitting up, crawling, or walking late. Talking late or having trouble with talking. Slow to master things like potty training, dressing, and feeding himself or herself. Difficulty remembering things. Inability to connect actions with consequences. John was thirty years of age when I met him, and Betty still had to toilet, bathe, and dress him. He was capable of feeding himself, but often I saw him being fed to hurry up the process so she could get on with the next job. He was a big guy, and on our trips together, with John sitting in the back seat, stomping his feet and yelling "no home, no home," the situation sometimes became scary. I thought he might put his foot right through the floor.

I took the lead from Betty in many areas of life, but she took the lead from me in trying to bring change in the area of disability rights. We joined many committees together, and our combined voices were heard, even though our ideas were not always accepted. People looked to us for advice and often thought we were mother and daughter. One woman made the comment, "Are you lesbians?" We just roared with laughter.

With the back-and-forth visiting, we got to know each other's families very well. Our lives were intertwined. Shopping, coffee out, and phone calls to each other were a normal part of our day. And all of this, just because I had stepped out and started a little group, looking to find a way in the wilderness. My life became richer, and the old saying "two heads are better than one" proved true. We provided each other with information and strength, and we also helped to carry each other's burdens—not physically, but with words. Each of us was very much her own person, with wisdom gained through many years of experience. When it all got too much, we shared our thoughts that suicide was an option, but neither of us took that road. These experiences were never shared with anyone else. We understood that it was a sacred trust.

Around this time John thought to make good use of our family home, he would raise the house on acro props and build in underneath to give more room for our growing family. Every weekend was taken up with this new project. He knocked out the posts on the perimeter and replaced them with the props, which could then be levered up or down to ensure the house was level and ready for the next stage. The year the house was raised, we had undue wet weather in May and June. The ditch which John dug by hand on the perimeter of the house for the foundation, filled with rain water overnight and by morning, some of it had started to cave in. Worried that we would lose the house, he hired a pump to drain the water from the trench and had a truck bring in blue metal. We ran backwards and forwards with barrow loads of the blue metal to fill the trench, to stablize the foundation and save the house from toppling over. Then, when the rain had passed, all the blue metal had to be dug out, and concete poured in to give the solid foundation to the house. A major project, and one which went on for several years, which included the outer perimeter of the house being bricked in, a new skin of concrete for the floor was poured, and plans made for an office, downstairs bathroom and laundry.

Upstairs, with the lifting of the house, walls had cracked, so that was an added expense. Four new rooms were added. A beautiful tiled bathroom, with a roman bath inlaid with bronze/gold tiles, large mirror and vanity basin.

The kitchen needed a remake, so cupboards, bench tops and the latest microwave oven were installed. A family room gave extra space for the family to relax and the floor tiling for these beautiful new rooms was done by John. The lounge had a bay window installed, and new drapes and carpet finished the elegant look of our new home.

CHAPTER 9

Rachel's Birth

Even though I was a busy mother of three children, I yearned for another baby. I felt I had the family on an even keel and was balancing my life successfully. I had always volunteered my time at my children's school, I had been a religious education teacher, I'd set up the support group, and now I looked forward to being pregnant again. It happened so quickly, I was amazed. In the early years of our marriage, when my husband and I travelled around Australia in a caravan, I would haunt all the churches with prayers to have children. It was a fear that I would be passed by. I don't know where that came from.

I stepped down from my outside commitments and enjoyed the pregnancy. It was a wonderful time. In March of 1982, with John present at the birth, and after a tiring labour, I was handed my new baby. As the doctor knew of my family's history of cleft palate, the first thing he did was to check her and give the okay that everything was all right. I was so relieved. I sat on the edge of the bed and couldn't decide between the names Rebecca and Rachel. Settling on Rachel, I went to sleep.

Waking up through the night, I discovered that I was haemorrhaging. I called a nurse, as I wanted to go to the toilet. She told me to get up and go. I tried—and fell to the floor and fainted. A nurse helped me back to bed, and an injection was given to stop the bleeding.

The next day, I noticed that my baby had a yellow tinge to her skin. The doctor rushed her back to the nursery to put her in a humidicrib, and a special light was turned on to help with her problem. Too much bilirubin had built up in her liver—so there she was, with a pair of goggles on to protect her eyes, basking in this light. We had a cross in our bloods during pregnancy, but after a couple of days, she was out of the nursery and back in my arms.

Kate was so overjoyed with the new baby. She made a huge banner that stretched around the lounge room, and when I arrived home with Rachel, she invited all the neighbours in to share in our joy. She just loved her little sister and would often take her out in the pram for a walk up the street while I rushed to cook tea. Often I had to call Kate back so the baby could have her bath.

My happiness spilled over into every part of my life. I now felt I was moving forward to the best of times, and I had realized my dream. I embraced this new change, and nothing seemed to worry me. Even a sinus condition that had bothered me suddenly cleared up, and my future looked bright. I felt God had rewarded me for achieving against impossible obstacles and odds.

Rachel's early years were wonderful for me. She was a baby who achieved the milestones easily, and I looked on in wonderment. Kindergarten and school came next, and I enrolled her at the local school the other children had attended. There was a gap of seven years between Jeffrey and Rachel, and twelve years between Kate and Rachel. Kate was always going to be the big sister, and not until later, when Kate went off to Brisbane to university to finish her studies, did I see how much Rachel missed her. It left a big gap in her life.

Rachel was a sensitive child, and I soon had to go to the school to sort out a bullying incident with another child in her class. Thankfully, the teacher understood and resolved the issue. Rachel finished primary school and went on to high school. She remained a quiet and thoughtful child.

In 1986, my husband went into business for himself, so that relieved a lot of the pressures with money. To go shopping for food and not have to take a calculator with me was heaven. Four children at private schools was costly but well worth the investment. We also had the pleasure of owning a beach house so we could take the pressure off family life and business.

By the time Rachel had entered grade ten, there were many changes happening in the family. Kate was married, Jeffrey was coming and going with out-of-town jobs, and my health was once again in decline. After a couple of years of heavy bleeding, it was evident that I would have to have a hysterectomy. I was rushed to the hospital after another heavy bleed with blood clots as big as my fist coming away. In accident and emergency, my blood pressure plummeted, so injections were given to me to stabilize my condition.

A day or so later, an Indian doctor came and said, "You have to have surgery, you can't go on like this." So within six weeks, surgery it was, but my health was so low. I was operated on in the morning, but I didn't wake until late in the afternoon. In addition to removing all of my reproductive organs, they'd had to do a lot of scraping of endometriosis off other organs in my body. I now wonder how I was able to have children in the first place.

My recovery was slow and painful. Jeffrey had moved to Toowoomba to go to university, and travelling down with what he needed to set him up in his location left me exhausted. My health did not improve. My husband blamed the hysterectomy for the change in our lives together. He felt that the sudden loss of oestrogen after surgery and the antidepressants I was now on to help me cope had caused a major breakdown of our intimate life. If I hadn't had the surgery, however, I have no doubt I wouldn't have survived. I was damned if I did and damned if I didn't. Shortly after, I crashed. Body, mind, and spirit went spiralling down, and there was nothing I could do to save myself. As I stood in the middle of the shopping centre, I felt life draining from me, like I was on a greasy pole and the only way was down.

During this painful time, I got in touch with a naturopath who lived a fair distance away, and Rachel and I drove down to meet with him. We stayed at a motel to start with, and then friends said we could stay at their beach house. I didn't feel as though the pills the naturopath was giving me helped me. He also treated Rachel, for she was going through her own stresses at the time and having trouble coping with what was happening at home. After a few sessions, I stopped going. Rachel felt he was just treating us with sugar pills.

Thoughts about my mother kept coming up, even though she had died ten years earlier. I rang the hospital, and they put me in touch with a therapist who was trained in gestalt therapy. I saw him for a period of nearly two years, and during that time the early years with my mother started to come up. I was shocked when he said, "She hid from you," meaning that when she couldn't cope with what was going on in my life at the time, she just turned away and was silent. It was a shock. What mother hides from her children? I had to come to terms with the fact that this was how my mother coped.

I had come to believe so strongly in the importance of family values, so I guess I knew it all along. Without realising it, I had chosen a path of embracing change and giving my family a better life than what I had known. Again, this is not to cast blame, but as we open up the past, we have to be ready to see things in their proper light. The truth does set us free, but we have to be willing to face it and embrace the pain. Only then can we move forward and leave the baggage behind. Love must enter and take the place of anger and resentment, or all that you will be left with is bitterness. I am grateful for all the memories my mother left me, the sweet ones and the ones I had to endure. They have made me the person I am today. To live a life of passion requires determination, courage, and the ability to stay the distance and realize your dream.

CHAPTER 10

Lourdes at High School

Lourdes' primary-school days were over, and it was clear that the only high school which could help her with her learning was on the other side of town. She was enrolled and settled in. She made some great friends who often came to stay for the weekend. It was wonderful that she was able to do this; not every student with her type of disability could.

But as the year progressed, there was clearly something wrong. She started to withdraw again. I was called to the school by the head teacher, who begged me to get her some help. I was confused; I thought that was what I had been doing all along. Meanwhile, during our meeting, Lourdes ran out of the school and off up the street.

"Go after her," said the teacher, "but please go and see your doctor."

"He's not interested," I replied.

"I don't care, just go," she said, explaining that perhaps the stress of a new school and a new curriculum was all too much.

For once, the doctor listened intently. He said, "She needs help, but to get it, you have to go to the city." It was there that a range of psychologists and social workers would try to get her to open up about how she was feeling.

At the same time, her orthodontia treatment had come to a standstill, as the work that was being done to bring her top jaw forward, in line with her bottom jaw, was detrimental to her. The device being used looked like an iron cage on her face. It was ugly and drew attention to her wherever she went.

I rang the plastic surgeon who had done Lourdes' surgery and asked his opinion. "That man is a big frog in a little pond," he said of the orthodontist we had been using. "You have to come to the city to get better results." Just add it to the list, Katherine!

The first trip to the city was horrific, with Lourdes dissolving into temper tantrums and running away into shops. I was exhausted. I knew I couldn't go on like this, so on the spur of the moment, I asked the orthodontist, "Can I get some help to fly down?" Each trip was five to six weeks apart. He looked at me with disgust. "How dare you? There is nothing wrong with your child. If you came in here with a kid who was puking all over the place, I would understand."

I walked back down to the city centre, found a phone box, and rang the child psychiatrist who was seeing Lourdes. "Come back to the hospital, I will help you," she said. She signed the appropriate forms for me to be able to make the trip every month or so, an hour in the air each way instead of a ten-hour bus trip each way. Bless her.

And so started a new routine that would last two years. Catch the 6.50 a.m. flight, see the range of specialists, walk down to the mall, have lunch, walk up to the clinic for the afternoon appointment, walk back to the city, catch a cab out to the airport, and wait for the next flight home. By eight in the evening we would walk in the door exhausted, me with a splitting headache. Thankfully, my husband had cooked tea, so we ate in silence and fell into bed exhausted.

At the beginning of this new program, I sometimes had to stay over the weekend. A friend let me stay with her and her family, but once again, Lourdes' behaviour, which was her way of telling me she was out of her comfort zone, intruded. My friend made it clear that if my daughter didn't stop "playing up," we would be asked to leave. I was so embarrassed.

During this time, my husband was running his own business and was stressed out, and I was leaving behind a sixteen-year-old, eleven-year-old, and four-year-old. I know my husband was trying to make sense of his new direction in life, but again I felt like I always had to be at the cutting edge of this massive change in our lives alone.

By the end of the first year of taking trips to the city, I was fed up, not seeing progress with Lourdes, and wondering why I was doing all this. I spoke harshly to the psychiatrist, who said she would write a letter to my husband to see if he could come down with me, at least now and then. The letter duly arrived, asking him to give some time to helping Lourdes and I with this new load being placed on us—and finally, a diagnosis of her condition as depression. It had taken a whole year and me having a little hissy fit to finally bring it all to a head. Antidepressants were prescribed and were a godsend in helping to lift her mood.

Also added was a new ear, nose, and throat specialist, the kindest of men, who absolutely knew how to handle Lourdes. She needed new grommets, and he even made the trip to our hometown to do her surgery. A new era of specialists from the city, coming to our hometown had opened up, and was I grateful. This doctor knew that she had a high pain tolerance, and so he got her to climb onto the operating table and have her grommets inserted without anaesthetic. I was impressed. Lourdes took it all in stride.

Halfway into the second year, on one of my visits with Lourdes to the specialists, my husband came with me on the trip. Whilst walking back from the dental clinic, I once again experienced pain and pressure in my chest. For several months, I had felt this discomfort on and off, but I had put it down to stress. I told the others to go on ahead to the mall while I sat at a chemist's shop, trying to recover. A few days later, I had another attack at a party, this time accompanied by vomiting, diarrhoea. and profuse sweating. I lay on the floor, not knowing what was happening.

At the hospital, my doctor came in and informed me that I'd had a heart attack. Next day, my urine turned black, and it wasn't long before a diagnosis of gall bladder problems was added. Apparently, my gall bladder had all but rotted away. Surgery followed, but a couple of days into recovery, I discovered I couldn't use my legs. This eventually passed; a nerve in my leg had been pressing against the sheet and that cut off all feeling. The cut across my stomach was so big, from one side to the other, that I jokingly said to the doctor, "Should have put a zip in it?" No smile, no sense of humour. Ah well, you can't win 'em all.

This brought an end to the trips to the city, and I was glad. Lourdes and I both needed time out from the constant running.

By the end of 1987, Lourdes was showing behaviour problems that I couldn't address, so a psychologist came to our hometown. I had just come out of surgery and was barely able to straighten up from the pain. We had been asked to bring in the whole family for the consultation, and this guy, in all of his wisdom, proceeded to emotionally tear the family apart. It was like hanging all the dirty linen on the line. He had the whole family in tears.

I stomped out the door, so angry. His suggestion was that we should send Lourdes to a psychiatric hospital and bomb her to her eyeballs with pills while she thought about her behaviour. I was appalled. "How could she think about anything?" I asked my friend. "And what about the other crazies there? She will be too vulnerable."

My friend calmed my fears. "Never forget, you are the child's mother. You make the final decision."

Armed with this advice, I was ready for the doctor on the next visit. When he swished into the room, dressed in long pointed black shoes and a type of black cape, I almost laughed in his face. I sat and told him, "None of what you suggest is going to happen. In fact, I don't like your attitude at all." With that, I got up and left the room with my husband trailing behind. It was the first time I had ever been rude to a specialist, but I wasn't going down a path that would lead to more problems. With no real answer in sight, it was carry on as usual, and hopefully answers would come.

To complete Lourdes' orthodontic work, I found a orthodontist locally who was willing to take on and finish what had been started several years before. At first, he suggested that bone might have to be taken from her ribs and attached to her jawbone; as with her cleft palate, the top jaw was not in line with the bottom jawline. I heaved a sigh of relief when the bands he placed around her teeth, with ever increasing pressure, proved to be doing the work. The government was helping to pay some of the costs under the cleft-palate scheme, so it was more affordable.

Towards the end of the treatment, the orthodontist called me into his surgery, and with tears in his eyes told me how courteous my daughter was each time she visited him. I was curious about his comment. He then went on to explain that he had many clients whose parents were wealthy and wanted their kids' teeth to look perfect, and not one of them ever bothered to thank him for his help. A few little words of appreciation meant so much to him, and coming from my daughter, they were all the more special.

CHAPTER 11

Job Training

High school years were over. Lourdes had graduated from grade ten, an academic achievement that had never been envisioned. Dressed in white, with pink roses in her lovely swept-up auburn hair, she looked stunning.

Reality soon struck, however. Now there was no need to get out of bed to catch the bus to school, so bed is where she stayed. It started to grate on my nerves, knowing it wasn't good for her to be lying around all day with nothing to do. An idea flashed through my head: "Maybe if she had something to take care of, it would help." With some phone calls, I was led to a lady who lived out of town and bred Burmese cats. This breed of cat is very dog-like in its behaviour, very loyal, and beautiful to look at. So Zachariah, a cute kitten, came to live with us. Slowly, with much coaxing and cajoling from me, Lourdes came to be a pet owner. If she ran out of cat food, she had to go to the corner shop and buy more, though sometimes I think my canned tuna found its way to the cat's bowl.

Zachariah was a chocolate Burmese and won first prize at the local show. It was a real effort to get there—up at five in the morning, make sure the white curtains for the cat cage are ironed, get everything into readiness for the big event. Once there, we wandered around, looked at the other cats, waited for the judges to make their decision, and headed home late in the day. It gave Lourdes something to talk about.

Unfortunately, Zachariah went missing not long after, so another cat was bought to take his place—another Burmese, lilac this time, and back to the show for another event. Raphael was a real winner; he took first prize at his first show and at the next, he won again. I was not really in love with the process—it was rather boring—but if it helped Lourdes (I hoped it was helping, anyway), then that was what we did.

Time was weighing heavily, with no progress on the home front. I arranged a meeting with a lady who was involved with disability, not really taking a lot of notice of the young girl sitting in the room with us. After the meeting, she chased after me to the car park and said, "You look like someone who has a lot of get up and go. Are you interested in meeting someone who helps kids who fall through the cracks?" Even though I was sceptical, I went to the meeting and listened to the man's ideas of getting together a group of like-minded people from various agencies who could help make a difference in the lives of young adults with a disability. I jumped on the idea. This was Lourdes' ticket to freedom. Well, sort of.

Often, the meetings consisted of only the two of us, and I suppose he must have thought that if he didn't do something, I wouldn't turn up either. He then brought in a woman from the city who was heavily involved in the training and employment of young adults—specialized programmes that got them into the workplace. This was what I had been waiting for, and I pushed hard to get it going. Approximately eighteen months later, CQ Personnel came into being, and Lourdes was its first client.

The training consisted of learning how to handle money, bag up groceries, smile at the customer, and so on. By 1991, we had purchased a beach house and would spend every weekend there. It was such a relief to get away from the everyday cares and worries, walk on the beach, and create a garden. It was heaven.

Well, the heavens had other ideas. They opened up to one of the biggest floods our little town had ever seen. We found we couldn't get back home, as the roads were flooded over, so we stayed put and watched the Gulf War in Iraq on TV.

With training over, a job placement at a supermarket was found. In her lovely uniform and navy blue stockings, Lourdes looked the picture of a checkout chick. She managed the job very well, but unfortunately, no backup was given on how to handle sarcastic remarks by other staff, bullying, or the politics of the workplace. She was extremely sensitive to all of this and often came home crying. I went out of my way to shop there, even though it was on the other side of town, pushing my trolley up and down the aisles and checking on her out the corner of my eye.

When we open up a new world, it brings with it the challenges of romantic relationships. Even for the average teenager, this is complicated; for someone who doesn't tick all the boxes, it is especially hard. One guy had his eye on her, but he showed his true colours when he appeared at the hospital where she was having surgery for an abscess and the staff found him in bed with her, taking the opportunity to get intimate. I am very sure she liked the attention—what young girl wouldn't?—but this wasn't love, even though she thought it was. So vulnerable. When he broke it off six months later, she was devastated.

We had an electrical business that we ran from home, and the phone was our lifeline—but now Lourdes was obsessive about trying to get the relationship back, and she made as many as fifty calls a day, really harassing the guy. She was powerless to stop. Depression set in, and she was a very unhappy girl with a broken heart.

She went missing one night, so we went out in the car looking for her. When I saw her, I hardly recognized her. She was distraught and her hair was in a tangle. Obviously, she'd been turned away again by that heartless guy. These were the times I questioned my decision to help her make a go of her life. It was like a knife through my heart. I agonized over it all.

Around this time, I happened to meet with a doctor who specialized in treating people with autism. I described the eccentricities my daughter exhibited, and he said, "I think we are talking about Asperger's autism. Make an appointment with me, and we'll go from there."

The appointment was seven hundred kilometres away, but it had to be done. The first time Lourdes met with him, she was scared, not knowing what to expect, but consecutive appointments clearly showed that they got on very well—even cracking jokes as they walked into his surgery. Another piece of the puzzle was in place. It only took nineteen years!

Kate had been working at an education centre. She rang me excitedly one day and said, "Mum, I've found a document written by a specialist, and it's all about Asperger's autism. Do you want to see it?" Immediately I knew we had found a key to unlock the mystery. I sat downstairs in the pergola, where I wouldn't be disturbed, with a coffee and tried to absorb the information before me. It was overwhelming. I rang my friend, Betty, distressed about what I had found. She said, "So now it's got a name, but your daughter is still the same person." She was right. A lot of the information related to what I had already lived through, so why was I so scared?

We took another trip to the city to see the specialist to get a prescription for antidepressants, and he also diagnosed Lourdes as having obsessive compulsive disorder. This explained the behaviour with the phone calls. Around this time, Kate—who was in a relationship with Geovani, a young Italian guy from Melbourne—wanted to go on a holiday together to Adelaide. Lourdes got it into her head that she was going and obsessed about it constantly. She went missing one night from the beach house, so I scoured the beach, hoping my worst fears wouldn't be realized. Kate and Geovani were leaving, so I asked them to check, just in case somehow she had made it home. They found her asleep downstairs. She had let herself into the house and just crashed with exhaustion after walking five kilometres to the edge of town and then hitching a ride with a stranger for the fifty kilometres back home. I didn't know whether to cry or be mad—both, I think. Some kind-hearted soul was in the right place at the right time.

Every person is an individual, and not everyone with Asperger's exhibits the same behaviour. Some behaviours were still unexplained, but the foundation that had been laid was standing her in good stead. All the years of doctors, therapies, surgery, specialists, and medicine certainly was not a normal way to live, but these things were necessary to give my daughter quality of life.

CHAPTER 12

Advanced Training in Disability

I decided to do a two-year advanced course in disability, with twelve modules, to see what the latest thinking was in this arena. I topped the class in behaviour modification, which spurred me on to keep going. Often I was a little late getting to class—sometimes five to ten minutes—as there was the family evening meal and other chores to do. This irked the teacher, who seemed to want a full explanation. I thought an apology was sufficient, being a mature-aged student.

One evening in class, one of my fellow students was left in tears as the teacher ranted and raved at her for some minor misdemeanour. I stood up for my friend and said, "I feel your criticism is too harsh. There is no need to reduce her to tears."

"We are all adults here," the teacher replied, "and should be treated as such."

As this lady was teaching ethics, I felt her approach was dictatorial. It didn't fit with the code she was sharing. My classmates felt the same, and they nominated me to approach the student council. I did, but there was no response.

When exam time came, she showed her true colours. Several in the class clearly hadn't passed, but she hurried them out the door. She waited until they had gone and then turned her full fury on me. I handed in my paper; she looked it over and said, "Well, you passed, but I don't want you to pass, so you will do this exam all over again."

I was floored. I wanted to get credits for my work, so I quietly asked, "What do you want me to write?"

She looked at me for a minute or so, knowing I was not going to cry about it or get upset. "Okay," she said, "here is what you will write." I copied word for word what she said. When the paper was done, she took it from me. As she walked away, I asked her to print me a copy. Minutes ticked by until eventually she emerged and handed me a copy that showed her rage. She had screwed up the paper and then had to flatten it out again to do the copy. I passed the exam for a second time, her behaviour was to make an example of me, as she resented my speaking up for a fellow classmate. I thanked her calmly, picked up my bag, and walked out of the room. I wondered why people like that went into this type of education. Surely one would like to feel that a good contribution had been made to students entering the field of disability. It is a tough industry to be in; one's heart has to be in the right place so that the people you work with are uplifted and supported. I have seen some disability workers with a heart of gold, and I have nothing but praise for them. Yes, at times we all get frustrated—trying to push forward when the person is not ready to take the next step—and I had to learn that lesson also. We get carried away with our own agenda.

To watch support workers still toileting and wiping dribble from the faces of adults and spoon-feeding them is to know that this is heroic work that rarely gets recognized. It is all done behind closed doors, but the ones who *do* know are the families who place their loved one in care because they can no longer do the work. To see a worker pass by a client and share a joke and smile is amazing. To do this day after day takes a special person. I know I couldn't do it—my life has been tough enough dealing with autism— but I suppose you learn to embrace whatever is handed to you. Betty and I talked about how she couldn't do what I did, and I knew I couldn't do what she was forced to do. What's the old saying, "God gives you what he knows you can handle"? Sometimes I think he overestimated me.

CHAPTER 13

❧❧❧

Oral History and Memories of the Orphanage

I saw an ad in the paper saying, "Do you have a story to tell about disability?" I approached my friend Betty, because I knew her story was so worth telling. At first she said no; she didn't want to dredge up painful memories. I told her I was willing to tell my story, so she finally agreed. It was an oral history, so I took my tape recorder to her place, and we sat down to reminisce about her early years with John, her disabled son. Hers was a story of courage and deep commitment to a son, her firstborn, who required lifelong support and personal care. Bathing, toileting, feeding, dressing, shaving—everything we take for granted that our children will grow up to do for themselves, she did for him.

He didn't walk until he was six years old; she carried him everywhere. She was told he would never walk, as his feet were too twisted—he had cerebral palsy—but she persevered in his exercises, and he did eventually walk, with the aid of heavy boots specially made for his feet. I can still see her going out to meet the bus that John came home on, helping him up the driveway, and dropping his bag on the step whilst he flopped into his easy chair. Then off with the boots, and afternoon tea was served.

It took me several weeks to record the story and type up the manuscript, but I fitted it in with my daily round of what I had to do. As her story was quite long, I decided my story would be in the form of a short poem. As the time for the publication of the book, *The A-Z of Disability*, approached,

I enquired as to whether everything was in place for the manuscript to be included. "No!" was the reply. "We don't have it. Are you sure you submitted it?" I called the co-ordinator of the program, who finally admitted that she had kept it back because it was such a good story, and she was going to publish it herself.

As my daughter Kate was living in the city at the time, she offered to go and collect the manuscript from the co-ordinator's office. With reluctance, the woman handed it over. It was submitted in time and appears in the book. A copy is in our council library.

When several writers came to my home to interview Kate and I about living with a person with a disability, the process was short and was basically a quick overview of Lourdes' life. They were looking for an older sibling's perspective on how she viewed family life.

Then the question was asked of me, "If it was all so hard, why didn't you give her up?" The words shot out of my mouth before I could think: "Because I had been given up, and I couldn't do it to one of my own." After they left, I was shocked to realize how that had stayed buried for so long.

I closed my eyes, and I was transported back in time to the year 1948. I was standing at my mother's knee. I was three, and she was sitting in the waiting room at the orphanage. I was crying and begging her to take me home. It was no use; she didn't answer but just looked very sad. Then she was gone. My sister and I were there because our mum could no longer take care of us. Our father had left—gone who knows where—and was not coming back.

In the dining room, I was seated at a long table—it was breakfast time—and an aboriginal woman was staring at me. I had long platinum blonde hair, so maybe that was the reason. All I knew was that I was scared and I wanted to go home. I wandered out of the orphanage. Near the kitchen was a pawpaw tree, and it was flowering. The smell was overpowering. Looking across the plain, I saw a train passing. I thought, "If I can just catch the train, then I can go home." But it was gone, and I was not on it.

There was a small shed out the back, and we were taken there to have clothes fitted. They put this itchy, scratchy tartan dress on me, and I hated it. I don't know how long I was there; it could have been three months.

I am not sure. I became very ill with grief, so they sent for my mother to come and see me. As she was still unable to take care of us, her visit was short and then she left. I remember a big open room with a lot of beds in it. My sister pushed her bed next to mine, so that she could be close to me during this difficult time.

To have this experience in life was an embarrassment to me for a long time. I cringed when a family member openly told my boyfriend that we had been in an orphanage. It was like a big dark secret not to be discussed. The feeling of being different was best kept hidden. For a long time, I didn't like second-hand clothes when they were offered to me and politely refused them. Nowadays, the experience no longer has that effect on me. If I see something nice in an op shop, I buy it. And I have found, over the years, that the painful memory of pawpaw flowers has gone. Today, I am just grateful there were people who cared for me when my family was in crisis.

CHAPTER 14

❧❧❧

1995: A Social Problem

*O*ne afternoon, a young aboriginal boy knocked on my door to ask, "Can I mow your lawn, lady?" Impressed that he was willing to earn some pocket money, I agreed.

After getting him started on the front lawn, I came back upstairs to be met by my son, who said, "Mum, why are you letting him do that? Those kids steal from everyone. There are usually two of them." I went downstairs, and sure enough, the other young lad was scouting around in the downstairs office, looking to help himself to whatever he could find. Apparently, it was common knowledge in our neighbourhood about these kids. I asked them both to leave. Days later, my milk money went missing, so obviously it was true. Not wanting to believe the worst, I just let it go.

As I came home from school one afternoon after picking up Rachel, a neighbour approached me about a neighbourhood meeting to be held in the church hall. She asked if would I come, saying, "You are the right sort of person we need to get this sorted out." Not really knowing the full extent of what she was talking about, I decided to attend the meeting. I was surprised to see how quickly the hall filled up with people from around the neighbourhood who had been robbed by these children. I didn't know the half of it.

An elderly lady who lived opposite one child's family was too scared to come down out of her house, so she stayed housebound for six months. I was shocked. Others told stories of the kids climbing two stories to reach a toilet window and gain entry into the house that way—even running past the occupants of the house while they were watching TV. I couldn't believe it!

After listening to the stories, I felt sure there would be a big committee of people who wanted to solve the problem. As it turned out, the big committee was me. Following the meeting, a neighbour who lived a couple of doors away approached me and said he would help. What had I gotten myself into? I didn't know where to start. What I did know was that the fact that these were aboriginal children made it a touchy subject. But I felt for the elderly who were frightened and trapped in their homes.

I approached the police, and they put me in touch with an aboriginal group. I attended one of their meetings, and after putting across my point of view, I asked, "What can you do to help?" I was met with a frosty silence.

Finally one lady answered, "Well then, you had better get the boy charged." As he was only twelve years old, that didn't sound like a good idea.

Inviting some aboriginal elders to my home for morning tea, I was shocked to hear that in a town further north, if the kids played up, they were taken out into the bush and belted. I was up against the age-old problem of the whites against the aboriginals. I spent many hours talking to the police in the hope that they could shed some light on the problem. Meanwhile, the stealing escalated, and I was continually hearing new stories of the children's escapades. Two boys would ride in a taxi and then, while one distracted the driver, the other robbed him, rolled underneath the car, and got away.

There had to be more to this than I understood or knew. Soon, stories of the kids' glue-sniffing emerged, and it seemed the parents of the boys involved were not going to help in any way, except to walk down my street, hand in hand, to give the appearance of a loving family. It was all a sham.

The ombudsman came to town. Our grievances were documented, but nothing was done. The police felt their hands were tied, as they didn't want to stir up racial problems. One nun came to me and told how her empty purse was handed back to her by the mother of one of the boys. "Sorry" was not going change the situation; there had to be support from government departments who were clearly failing in their duty to help these boys.

I just laughed when one government official covered it all up by saying, "Oh, you poor boy, you were forced to go out and steal. The bus didn't come by and pick you up for your outing."

The government sometimes had meetings in different towns, and by sheer chance they came to our town. I asked for a meeting with one of the ministers who I thought would give me a chance to put our views across and be heard. In the meantime, we had been writing letters to different departments, from the premier down, who we thought might just listen to us. It was a siege mentality. These kids were running rampant in the community and nothing could be done. The letters were either not answered or a curt "We'll look into it" was the only reply.

A few weeks before the meeting, there was an article in a national magazine on how the aboriginal women of this country were fed up with the drinking problems and the abuse from their men. The women had marched bare-breasted down the main street of Alice Springs to show their solidarity and rebellion against the problems they were facing. I salute them. They also were brave enough to say, "The handouts from the white man will not solve these problems. We have to solve them ourselves. No amount of money is going to do it. It is an aboriginal problem." I took these facts to the meeting, but I wasn't heard. Later, I was told that I was too uptight.

We had many meetings with our member of parliament and often rang him when we knew parliament was sitting. Nothing. It was then decided to get all parties together, and hopefully a resolution could take place. In attendance were one inspector, three other high-ranking police officers, an aboriginal representative, our local member, and several interested parties, including my neighbour and myself.

I spoke of the frustration of having our neighbourhood in virtual lockdown, with people afraid to go out in case they came home and found themselves robbed again. There was a general unease within the community. The police told me later they were impressed with my presentation, although the aboriginal representative felt we were just picking on the kids. It was frustrating to say the least. One lady who had no stake in it at all criticized me, saying, "You should be ashamed of yourself, those poor kids can't help it!" Mmm, she hadn't been robbed.

One morning, I rang a retired magistrate of the court, a well-respected man in the community whose job it was to listen to a case being presented and then hand down judgement as he saw fit. He was not a man to tangle with, and he told me, "The rights of the community come first. Perpetrators will be dealt with through the justice system." I was on the right track, but it didn't help that these thieves were underage.

Towards the end of the year, the premier of Queensland came to town, and my friend and I attended the morning tea. I spoke to his wife, hoping that as a woman and a mother, she would see my point of view. She listened, but she made no promises. A short time later, the inspector of police rang me one afternoon and said, "It is all over. The boy is being flown this afternoon by jet to a detention centre." I gave a sigh of relief but felt sadness for a boy who, in his short life, had never had the loving support he needed to get his life on track.

It was evening when a big truck with many aboriginals on board came up my street yelling and trying to intimidate me. It was all very stressful. I rang the inspector, who said, "Don't worry, it's all for show." I sometimes think back to that episode in my life and wonder if I could have done anything differently. I asked for help every step along the way, but fear ruled the day. With loving discipline, there might have been a successful outcome.

None of us know how our kids will turn out. We hope and pray that we have done enough of the right things for them to become good people who contribute to society in a positive way. If that happens, we are truly blessed. And I have no doubt that my words to the premier's wife found their mark, and she influenced her husband to do the right thing.

CHAPTER 15

❧❀❧

A Wedding for Kate and Motherhood for Lourdes

K ate and Geovani's wedding was in late 1995. She was a beautiful bride with a beautiful wedding party. Lourdes, Rachel and Jeffrey stood proudly beside their sister on her special day. Kate had hired a stretch limousine to take us to the church. Nothing like making a statement!

As we entered the church, John on one side of Kate and myself on the other, it was overwhelming that this happy day had finally come about. To my surprise, I glanced over at Geovani's family as I was walking down the aisle and saw them all dressed in black. The thought crossed my mind, *It's not a funeral.* I found out later that it is traditional in Italian culture to wear black at weddings. My outfit, which had taken a lot of choosing with the help of my friend, was a beautiful soft dusky pink dress. The bodice had small petals, one under the other, all the way down to the waist and the skirt, with soft filmy tulle over satin. If the wind had caught it, I would have looked like Marilyn Monroe in her famous picture standing on a grate as her skirt lifts up. Then again, I didn't have Marilyn's legs.

A midday ceremony followed the wedding breakfast and then we went down to the beach house to finish off the day with seafood platters. I am sure Geovani's family appreciated that gesture. Both his parents came to us in the kitchen and thanked us profusely.

Although I didn't know it then, at the time of the wedding Lourdes was pregnant. She had been seeing a guy on the quiet, and I noticed some mornings she wasn't well. Well, the news soon broke, and then she informed me that she was moving out of our home and going to live with her boyfriend. I hadn't even met him yet. *How on Earth is she going to cope, living away from home?* was my first thought, but there was no stopping her.

I visited the flat where they were living, and I was shocked. One dirty mattress and a freezer was all he possessed. I kept my composure. It wouldn't do to upset anyone at this stage, but I had a bad feeling about the situation.

Lourdes' first baby, Amanda, was born quickly and easily. Once again, Lourdes' high pain tolerance stood her in good stead. I was amazed, watching as she gave birth. One elderly nun who Lourdes knew from her school days visited her, chatting and praising her on being a mother.

Lourdes and her boyfriend moved to an old house that was once a presbytery, and then I started to notice changes in his behaviour. He became more aggressive and even showed open aggression toward me. I thought he was going to hit me. I was a grandmother for the first time and I wanted to support them, but it was clear I wasn't wanted.

Soon after, they decided to get engaged, so we went out of our way to make it a happy event. It was left to the family to keep up the pretence. Her boyfriend was off doing his own thing, eating away from the rest of us. I soon learned that he'd had a rough upbringing and had been tossed out onto the streets by the age of thirteen. His family didn't want anything to do with him. So what I was seeing were basic survival skills.

Amanda was christened at the local church, dressed in the beautiful white robe our children had been christened in. Lourdes and her fiancé kept moving, house to house, not staying very long in any one place. His behaviour escalated into open temper tantrums. One night he pushed Lourdes out of the house, locked the door, and told her not to come back. We were afraid for Amanda. What would he do to her? We had no choice but to call the police. With guns drawn, they entered the house and retrieved the baby. It was all very distressing, and it wasn't going to get better any time soon.

Lourdes had her second baby, Jessica, two years later, and by this time they had moved again. He liked to keep control of the money, to spend it on what he wanted—games, DVDs, and marijuana. At this time, a government agency was called in to help Lourdes with her babies, and I was told there wasn't enough food for the children.

One morning, I found one of my rings missing. My mother had beautiful polished sapphires that her father had mined out at Anakie many years before. In my mother's estate, these sapphires were left to share out amongst the three of us. I chose my mother's favourite, the golden one, which I had set up with diamonds in memory of her for Kate's wedding.

I knew he had asked Lourdes to steal the ring so he could pawn it. I went to the house and demanded it back. That was when Lourdes told me she was being mentally and physically abused. He would push her down onto the concrete floor and kick her. Oh Lord, what a mess.

I had no idea how this was all going to play out; all I knew was that she was in trouble. I urged her to leave him. One night, I took her to the place where a young girl had been murdered. Her life had been taken in a paddock in the heart of the city, hidden by long grass. Flowers had been placed on the fence—hundreds of bouquets. As we stood there in prayer, I begged Lourdes once more to leave her boyfriend, telling her what happens when we don't protect our own. "Do you want this to happen to you and the girls?" I asked. She didn't speak, just listened. We stood there for an hour or more, and then I took her home.

Next morning, very early, she was at my door with both babies in her arms. She stayed with us for several months and then drifted back into the relationship—with promises, no doubt, that he would treat her better. Again they moved house, like gypsies, always moving on. They moved to a cheaper rental across town, and the place was a mess. There were bags of rubbish everywhere. She came home one day complaining that once again, he had thrown her out of the house, this time having another woman stay with him for the night. She had slept on the footpath.

John and I went to the house and found that Amanda was locked in a bedroom, with her father blocking the door. We left, and the next day, they were gone. We rang his mother, and she claimed she didn't know where they were. I didn't believe her, so we drove out to her house, hoping to catch a glimpse of Amanda. Nothing. I was frantic.

We returned to the house to sort out Lourdes' belongings. The place was filthy, with dirty dishes, food scraps, and clothes piled just anywhere.

It had never been a home. We cleaned it up best we could and left the rest. I can only imagine the trauma that played out in that house.

For the next few weeks, we rang around people they knew, but no one was offering any information. I approached a solicitor for help. Little did I know that she had never tracked down an abducted child, so this was a test case. I had a photo of Amanda on my desk, but I found it too painful to look at it every day, so I put it away. My determination to find her, however, never wavered. I couldn't bear for her to be away from our family.

Months went by with no progress, or so it seemed. Back and forth to the solicitors, asking questions, hoping they would find a way to bring this beautiful child home. Meanwhile, Lourdes was deep in a gloomy mood.

Then, one day, out of the blue, there was a big booming voice on the end of the phone, asking for my details. They had tracked the father to a caravan park in Melbourne, and Amanda was still with him. Would I come to Melbourne on the next plane? I scrambled to get flights and told Lourdes, "You are coming with me. You are her mother. She needs you."

We flew to Melbourne, and as I entered the airport, I could see a very large man, looking very much like a cop, scanning the crowd. I walked past him and stood behind him. He turned around and said, "Are you Katherine Steele?"

I nodded, and he said, "Come with me, we have Amanda with us now." My heart was pounding, and then I heard this wail from around thirty metres away—"Nana, Nana, Nana!" I rushed over, and there was our little darling—poorly dressed, with her hair matted and filled with head lice. I thanked the police, and we walked away. I couldn't believe our luck.

We had brought a suitcase of fresh clothes with us. I tore off the dirty dress and replaced it with a fresh one, I didn't even wait to go to the ladies room. I couldn't do anything about her hair, so I just brushed it. The lice would have to wait until we got home. The plane flight is buried in my memory somewhere. All that mattered was that we had her back. It had taken a long eight months to find her and bring her home.

I have often wondered what happened to her during that time and what effect it will have on her as she grows up. Does she remember? One counsellor suggested she probably doesn't—maybe to placate me, or because the counsellor didn't want to get into it. Either way, I think this is wrong. We do store those memories, and they do come back to haunt us.

We arranged for Lourdes to live at an estate not far from us. It was owned by a church group and had a caretaker living on the premises. Every day I would go over to see how Lourdes and the girls were doing. As it turned out, not very well. I often found Lourdes in bed, depressed, with the children quietly playing with their toys. Once again I called in a support group agency to help with the housework and feeding the children.

Then, wouldn't you know it, the boyfriend turned up. He had tracked her down, and no doubt Lourdes had encouraged him. I thought she was over that part of her life, but obviously not. Apparently, he came and went, though I never saw him. They were fighting again, and the older residents complained. After about six months, we got her into a housing commission house just around the corner from us. His hold on her—not only because of the children but also his bullying ways, making her think he was taking charge and being "the man of the house"—kept the relationship going. Before long, she was pregnant for a third time.

Charlotte was born early in 2003, a tiny scrap of a being, weighing in at four pounds two ounces. The nurse commented, "Not cooked yet, send it back," making us laugh. Lourdes was a better mother to this child, and her days settled down to a rhythm of feeds, baby sleeping, and housework. Amanda was now seven and Jessica five, so they were of some help to their mother. Around this time, Lourdes' boyfriend started drifting out of her life. He had met another partner. I looked at all that had happened as a stepping stone to something better for her.

What a learning curve for both of us. I believe we have to stay in the arena of life long enough to have the riches dropped at our feet. When there are no backward steps, and life is testing, testing, and your back is against the wall, sooner or later a breakthrough comes. What a glorious time! It's like a brand new world. When the gift of new life is in our hands, the pain and suffering just melt away.

CHAPTER 16

❧❧❧

Ill Health

By now, my health was beginning to fail big time. The stress was taking its toll, and my relationship with John was on a downward curve. Late in 2002, I had the flu, which I treated with vitamin C. Lying in bed one afternoon, I started to see spiders everywhere. I closed my eyes, and the spiders were still there. I was hallucinating.

I got up to walk to the kitchen and found I could hardly move my legs. By evening, I rang Kate. Most concerned, she said, "Mum, get to the hospital straight away." John wasn't feeling very well either, but he drove the car to the hospital. We were both sent for X-rays, and as it turned out, we both had pneumonia. Coming back to the accident and emergency department, I was joking with the nurses. Over the years, I have developed a pattern of behaviour: when I feel unsure of myself, I use humour to lighten the load. Looking at me with a serious expression on her face, the nurse said, "You don't know how sick you are."

I was moved into a very small room that night. It felt like a broom cupboard, and then the next day, I was transferred to an isolation ward. I was still hallucinating, as strange conversations flitted in and out of my head. Doctors came and went, discussing their ideas of what to do with me, whilst all the time not really knowing what my condition was. At times, especially at night, I felt really low, so I prayed, "Lord, I'm not ready to go yet, help me."

My days were spent in pain, trying to get enough air. My lungs were full of fluid, so they operated on my back and inserted a tube into my lung, hoping that when they hooked it up to a pump, the fluid would come out. It didn't work. The procedure, even though I was given a local anaesthetic, was painful.

"What are you griping about?" one nurse said. "All the oldies don't complain."

I could hear the coughing coming from an adjacent ward. People who had smoked all their lives were now paying the price with chronic bronchitis and emphysema.

A South African surgeon—who I joked with about rugby by asking "Who is playing better, your team or ours?"—still felt his idea of surgery through my back was the best option. The other doctor wanted to airlift me to the city, where surgery would entail a huge cut under my lungs, from the front to the back. I don't think I would have survived that operation.

One afternoon, the surgeon was back with a team of doctors to operate on me again. This time, they would insert a tube the size of a garden hose into my lung. Thank God for my son-in-law, Geovani, who had done medical training with his radiography. He comforted me with, "Mum, you ask for a drug called midazolam. You won't really go out to it, you won't remember what is happening to you, and you won't feel pain either." He was right. When the anaesthetist administered the drug, I was out like a light

Half an hour later, it was all over. The large hose was in my lung, and the other end was connected to a portable carrying case. The fluid that was pumped out of my lung went into this device. I was expected to get out of bed straight away and walk down the hall carrying this case, but not let it get any higher than my heart, as the fluid would just drain back in. Well, I don't know about walking, I staggered along, holding onto the wall, and then collapsed back into bed, exhausted. Then the pain set in, and it didn't matter which way I turned in bed, everything just hurt. It was a difficult time.

My condition was called *empyema*, which means fluid has turned to a solid mass. I had to make sure I got a flu shot every year and a pneumonia shot for a couple of years. I looked so emaciated—I had lost eight kilograms in weight during my ten days in the hospital—and I was unable to stand. My darling daughter Kate came to look after me for two weeks, even though she had a new baby to care for. I know my family was shocked by my condition; I think I gave them a big scare. I took showers sitting on a chair and was encouraged to eat, even though I had no appetite. Ten steps out the back door was more than enough exercise, so back to bed to rest.

As I sat out in the garden one afternoon, my neighbour, who was a nurse, told me that the procedure I had gone through was very new. It took me nearly two years to regain my strength afterward. Reading up on empyema much later, I found that 70 per cent of people die a year or two after being diagnosed with this condition.

This was not the first time I had come close to losing my life. As a child, I was hit by a car and woke up to find my head wedged against the wheel, with the driver screaming, "I've killed her, I've killed her!" I have never remembered the actual accident, just getting up and riding off on my bike. Another time, I was admitted to hospital so ill I couldn't walk. The doctors thought it was polio. I was in isolation ward at the hospital for several weeks with injections round the clock to save me. I have at times wondered, *Why all this drama? Why doesn't my life just go smoothly?* There is no answer; either I accept my lot in life or not. But I do continue to wonder if there's a plan to all of this.

A spiritual friend of mine said, "It isn't your time to go yet." To feel uplifted, I turned to movies that inspire me, like *Mao's Last Dancer* and *Invictus*, and they left me with a feeling of admiration for the strength and courage of people whose lives have been impacted by tragedy yet still go on to greatness. I think Marianne Williamson summed it up beautifully in her book *Age of Miracles* when she wrote, "Now is the time to burst forth into your greatness—a greatness you could never have achieved without going through exactly the things you've gone through. Everything you've experienced was grist for the mill by which you have become who you are. As low as you might have descended, in God there are no limits to how high you can go now."

CHAPTER 17

❁❁❁

Disability in the Family

*I*t is always interesting to see how others respond when discussion turns to a family member who has a disability. I think it depends on the type of disability and the nature of the person responding. Genetics also plays a part. In all of this, it comes back to the family itself: Where did that child come in the mix? Was he or she the eldest, the baby of the family, or somewhere in the middle? How does each person respond to what is going on in the family at different stages of life? Do they think they got a raw deal, or did they deal with the problem successfully? Each person sees it differently.

My friend's son John was the eldest and the one with disability, and she always felt that the other children in the family accepted him for who he was and were very loving toward him. I have read articles on this subject, and quite a large percentage were okay with someone in the family who had a disability. I can only speak for myself and my situation.

We each bring to the table what we have learned in childhood and then decide, does this attitude serve me and others in bringing out the best in those around us? Some of us try to step up to the mark, while others bury themselves in work or avoidance. Human behaviour is such a complex subject, and change usually occurs slowly and oftentimes only when the pain of staying the same is too much. It is only then that a leap of faith into the unknown brings about a new way of living and relating to others.

To forge ahead takes courage and tenacity. We can all do new things on the spur of the moment, but to make permanent change, the behaviour has to be repeated over and over until it becomes a part of who we are. New neural pathways in the brain are opened up and the old ones die off eventually. Change can occur in an instant, but usually ninety days is the norm for this to happen. In the meantime, your mind is probably telling you it can't be done, but persistence eventually pays off.

That's how you learn to ride a bike. You fall off quite a few times before finally you let go of the fence which has been supporting you and then freewheel it down the street. All learning is a process—some of us hurry it up and some slow it down, depending on the circumstances, but when we bravely step outside our comfort zone, take the bull by the horns, and ride it for all it's worth, we are on the right track. The direction taken can be changed, but if the trajectory is upward and feels right, then you are on the right path.

To compare yourself to others is a mistake, and for others to criticize and condemn you when they have not been in your shoes is also a mistake. The path you take is measured by your own efforts and the benefits that eventually show themselves. Child-raising has been going on for eons, but the rights of people with disabilities have only come to the fore in recent times. Yes, there are societies who kill off a baby that is not perfect, but I like to think that as human beings, we have left those wretched ideas far behind.

To appreciate the changes in people who have a disability, you have to take the long view, like with a pair of binoculars. You see so much at a distance, but the steps to get there are hidden. It takes infinite patience, as their learning is a lot slower and their fears are even bigger than ours. How can we expect it to be any different?

To achieve change, one must stay in the trenches, in the heat of battle, willing to endure whatever it takes. This is built on the knowledge of a previous victory won with blood, sweat, and tears. No matter how small the win, it is to be celebrated.

On the normal path of growing up, parents look for and expect their children to reach certain milestones—that first smile, grasping a rattle, rolling over, sitting up, and crawling. From there, children typically move on to walking, running around, and exploring the environment. Photos are taken and carefully put into albums to be looked at again and again in admiration of the new addition to the family. I found no time for photos, nor did I want to record the agonizingly slow progress. Photos were taken, but not by me.

Etched in my memory are places where I deeply felt the pain of being on a different path from other mothers. I can still see the tree we sat under at the beach where I struggled to feed Lourdes, or her running in panic from the waves. Little episodes, but built into those memories is the sadness of knowing I was on the road less travelled. It was very lonely.

My one true friend in those early days, Tessa, was pure gold to me, with her total acceptance of who I was and my situation. Only someone who had been cast into the furnace to be purified—with the ego burnt out of her, leaving pure love—was good enough to journey with me. Others fell by the wayside with their scorn and hurtful remarks. I guess it left me lighter, to get on with the task of living and finding my way forward.

I know some mothers who found the load too heavy and handed their child over to a government institution. At the time I was aghast at their decision, but a time would come when I felt I couldn't go on, and then I understood. One weekend, totally fed up with temper tantrums and obnoxious behaviour, I drove Lourdes to a hostel with the intention of getting her a room. Just as I pulled up and wound down the window, wouldn't you know it, some old gentleman, boozy and unshaven, poked his head in and said, "Are you coming to live here? I live in the hostel." How could I leave her with that old derelict and Lord knows who else? I started up the car and went home. The answer didn't lie there.

Who knows the heart and mind of someone less fortunate than ourselves? We can't, unless we are shown by their behaviour or their words. I was absolutely blown away when the time came for Lourdes to make her first confession in our church. Later, the priest came and without telling me exactly what she had said, intimated that her confession went deeper than what most kids professed. There was a lot more going on in her heart and her soul than one would suspect.

My friend Betty's son, who was severely handicapped, learned to count the vinyl discs as they dropped down on the record player. No one taught him this; he worked it out for himself. So where does this intelligence lie that can stay dormant for many years and then show up out of the blue? I am always in awe of people whose journey has taken them over mountains that were supposed to never be climbed and rocky ledges that only a mountain goat would dare clamber up, and persist with their last ounce of breath to gain the view from the peaks they were told were impossible for them to reach. Bravo!

As adults, we have a responsibility to ourselves to make necessary changes in our behaviour if the old way no longer serves us. Bemoaning the fact that Mum or Dad didn't do the right thing and laying blame only serves to keep us in the victim mode. To forgive, knowing that no one is perfect, and then step up and embrace a new way of life does take courage, but it is well worth the effort.

CHAPTER 18

Main Players in My Life

*A*ll my life, I have been surrounded by people who instead of giving me the support I needed gave me emotional neglect. Instead of strong people, the ones I have attracted can't or won't step up to be there for me. This is not condemnation, just an observation of who the main players in my life have been. You can't give what you don't have. I know that. So, in essence, I have had to be the person I so desperately wanted others to be. This has been very hard for me to come to terms with. I know that having my father leave when I was three years old, and still having clear memories of him, has impacted my life.

The person I admire most from my very early years is my paternal grandmother. We lived with her for awhile as our house was being built. I remember her as a small Italian lady, strong in her faith and in her way of life. Grandfather was a shearer and had a liking for the drink. Grandmother wasn't waiting around to see her hard-earned savings go down the drain. Fed up, she packed up the buckboard and her two sons (including George, my father) and drove the horse-drawn carriage over the Drummond range to our little town, where she bought a house and told him, "When the drinking stops, you can join me." Woo-hoo, one strong lady. Maybe I took my direction from her.

She had lovely flower beds out in front of the cottage, and out in the back were herbs, grown in galvanized tanks, cut down to half their size. She sold bunches to the neighbours to make extra money. She grew veggies, kept chickens in the coop down the back, and had a grape arbour with a screeching cockatoo hanging up in a cage.

I remember the soups she made, even though I wasn't too keen on them—but as a two-year-old, what would I know? She always had a stern look on her face, and now I know why: she had to take the lead in the household. She ran her house like clockwork. Each day was set aside for particular allotted tasks—washing on Monday, ironing on Tuesday, baking on Wednesday, going to town and shopping on Thursday, visitors on Friday. And of course, Sunday was always Mass. Her life was regimented by the times. In the late 1940s, everyone did the same thing. But she did it well.

I can still remember picking flowers from the garden with her when I was two years old. I had pulled off all the leaves; she wasn't too pleased about that and let me know it. But she impacted me greatly with a desire for order in life and an ability to forge ahead in spite of difficult circumstances, put a stamp on life, and make a place in the world. She did not show affection, but I admire her greatly, even after all this time has passed.

When my parents divorced a few years later, I did not see her for many years, even though we lived around the corner from her place. A split in the family, in those days, was taken seriously, and never the twain shall meet. Once, when I was eighteen and working as a secretary, we passed on the street, and she stopped and said, "Hello, how are you, Katherine?" After a few more pleasantries, she went on her way. I never knew what kind of thoughts and feelings she had about how life had panned out for her. She died about six years later. My mother wrote to us about her passing, as we were then living in Victoria. It was the end of an era.

I often think back to those very early years of peace and tranquillity, and the photos of me taken at the time show that to be true. The pictures are of a very happy two-year-old with long platinum-blonde hair riding a bike, singing, and generally being at peace with the world.

CHAPTER 19

The Fork In The Road

As my strength came back, I took on more responsibilities in our business, often staying up late working on the computer—after a full day of housework and time spent supporting Lourdes and the girls so that their lives could stay on track. It wasn't easy.

One afternoon, late in 2004, John came home from work and said he wasn't well. I called an ambulance, and he was asked to lie down on the floor. The paramedics came in and attended to him, and next thing he was off to the hospital. It was a heart attack. As I sat with his brothers at the hospital that night, we were all in a sombre mood. He was to be airlifted to the city to have stents inserted into his heart.

I drove to the city with a friend in the car, as it was too far for me to do the trip by myself. A relief driver was a good idea. After about a week, when John's treatment was complete, he was released to come home. That emergency dash had saved his life. He no longer wanted to continue with his electrical business, so instead, he took a job out of town.

Depression often follows a heart attack, and around this time there was a big change in John's attitude toward me and the family. He was going through a midlife crisis and was very unhappy with his life. He had been on this path for some time, but as I believed in the importance of family values and had risen to face enormous challenges, I hoped we could resolve our differences.

One afternoon, he announced that he was leaving. He started packing his clothes and putting them into his vehicle. The family sat stunned in the lounge room until Lourdes calmly said the words I was incapable of saying. What she said struck to the heart of what was happening. I couldn't believe that she was capable of seeing the situation with such clarity. I was gobsmacked. As he left, I pulled down the garage door and locked it. My marriage and my way of life of forty years was over.

The first two years after John left, the anger that consumed me led to my clearing my home of anything and everything, that I no longer needed. Clearing away the clutter in my mind and in my home left space for me and what my life now consisted of. I was officially on my own after forty years of marriage, and even though I had done so many things in my life on my own, the transition was going to take a while. I was still in shock, and my friend Betty and I talked on many occasions as I tried to unravel what had happened. Her wisdom helped me greatly, and her words "business as usual" meant I was to carry on with my daily life as best I could.

I rediscovered Reiki, an energy healing that I had come across years before. I now wanted to immerse myself in its mysteries. I signed up for a weekend seminar and was taught the basic steps of Level 1 and Level 2. I was amazed when, on the second day, the Reiki master did healing on my hips, which had been causing me considerable pain for several years, and the pain disappeared. I share the gift of healing with anyone who asks for my help.

I also attended a spiritual group where I came across the teachings of self-liberation. This opened a door to looking at life in a different way. At first, I found it hard to understand this way of thinking, but with perseverance, a whole new world opened up to me. The group leader's words were, "You must learn to stop thinking in terms of beginnings and endings, successes and failures, and begin to treat everything in life as a learning experience." He showed me that when one door closes, another door does open. To yearn for the old life only brings more suffering, so "to stop the story, stops the bleeding." That brings a kind of peace in itself. Bathing in my salt pool and releasing my suffering skyward was also a ritual I used to move myself forward.

As I look back on my three score years and ten, I ask myself, "What have I learned?" Hopefully, I am more tolerant of others—live and let live. Gratitude has always been a part of my life, even for the small things. Forgiveness is in itself a gift, and I think throughout my life, I have tried to overlook others' mistakes. There does come a time when someone inflicts a pain that just doesn't go away. It gets deeper and deeper into one's soul.

I have not always been very good at speaking up for myself, often to my own detriment. I will speak on behalf of others, but I think my early training of "just put up with it" has seeped into my subconscious and left a wound. I remember my mother and I visiting a neighbour when I was around three years of age. I needed to go to the toilet, but I was not allowed to ask, until finally I couldn't wait any longer. I was ashamed to speak up, but when I finally did, it was met with, "Of course, it's okay." These are silly little things, but they shape our world.

My mother was a very shy person and came from a German background, where it wasn't polite to push yourself forward. Consequently, she missed out on situations where perhaps others could have helped her. I know my mother loved me very much, but she didn't show affection; that was something I had to learn as I went along.

Having come from an early life of disruption and a scarcity of food at times, I still say a quiet "thank you" when I am able to bring home the groceries. Back in my early days, things got so bad at one point that a neighbour asked St. Vincent de Paul to call on us to help out. The two men who came were neighbours and belonged to the Catholic Church; they served as support people for those in need. To come home to find a box of groceries on the front porch was a blessing. That went on for a year. I thought my mother was ashamed—it was hard to read her sometimes—but no, she was as grateful as I was.

Sometimes I still see one of those men when out shopping, and I have gone up to him and his wife, and yes, they remember me very well. I find that amazing, as he is in his nineties now. He and his wife had a big family of seven children. What selfless service!

Prayer has always been a part of my life. A spiritual awakening happened very early one evening. I was about ten years of age and my mother, stepfather, and I were gardening. All of a sudden, I fell on my knees in prayer. I don't know the why or how of it; it just happened. When I married, I embraced the Catholic faith, until an upheaval later in my life made me look further for a deeper meaning and a different path.

To look at one's life in the context of what has been achieved is only part of the story. The day-to-day living—where mistakes are made, tempers are lost, and you yell at the kids and your partner—is part and parcel of what it is to be human. Pressure builds, problems seem insurmountable, and yet we try to go on in spite of it all. I now see that the toughest times in my life are the gifts presented; how we cope is left up to us. Do we fall and get carried out of the ring, or do we rise and fight on, even when there is no end in sight? To see the smallest step as victory is an achievement in itself. I think those tough years in the trenches, when my back was often against the wall, have stood me in good stead to try to fight the good fight—and still have hope that things will get better.

CHAPTER 20

Reflections on My Life

I have now come to realize I was looking for the holy grail in life. How did I come to that conclusion? As I had plummeted to the depths of despair and worked my way back up from the black pit, to finally look over the top, I think I saw the stars and wondered what was possible. Although I didn't know it at the time, I was tapping into my potential and also my daughter's. Who knew what wonders lay there?

I was getting used to waiting for the smallest sign of change in her, which often took months or sometimes years. Her behaviour modification programme, which I implemented, showed little forward movement even after six years. Why didn't I give up? Was I just plain stubborn, or was something unknown to me urging me on? A nervous nature due to instability in my early life left me with high stress levels. Faced with *any* new situation, I would go through dry retching and lots of tears. But when someone's life depends on you, there is no choice but to move forward. Why didn't I just accept what was in front of me? Why go looking for something that was only going to cause me more pain? The answers lie buried in who I am.

I can remember, as a two-year-old, trying to push my grandfather's mower. I couldn't reach the handle and got myself into a hell of a tizzy because I couldn't make it happen. Isn't that silly? I loved the smell of fresh-mown lawn, to see the clippings fall in the bag at the back of the push mower, and I couldn't understand why I couldn't do the same.

I have always felt that it was important to go the extra mile to help others. Going to the shop around the corner from home to take eggs that my mother had promised the shopkeeper in exchange for lessening the bill was not a pleasant task. The shopkeeper's wife would announce to all those present, "Here comes that Jones kid again, looking for credit," and it embarrassed me. But my mother knew I would do it. It took her a year to pay off the bill. My stepfather was out of work, as the meat works had shut down because of strikes.

I can still see her filling out those hated forms for unemployment benefits. As her education was grade three level only, it was difficult for her. With my first job, my mother and I decided to buy ourselves each a bedroom suite and pay it off, which was allowed in those times. A sort of lay-by system, in which you got the goods upfront and then made regular payments until it was all paid off. No sooner was the furniture delivered than there was another strike at the meat works, and my stepfather was out of work again. The look on my mother's face prompted me to take her payment book with me so as to spare her the embarrassment of having to send the furniture back. That went on for a year. I guess she had an expectation of me that really was above and beyond what a normal teenager would do.

Basically I am a shy person, but I guess life has asked me, "Do you want to step up to the next level?" and even though I am uncomfortable at the time, I always say yes.

I think of my early life with my mum, my sister, and I. It was my duty to help where best I could. Today that is called codependency, but to just get by in those early years, I felt if we pulled together it would lessen the load. I have the gift of being able to put myself in another person's shoes, and all that I learned later came into play in my decisions regarding my daughter's welfare.

My mother urged me to take another job when I was nineteen. She thought the better pay would help. The job was an hour away from our town. I didn't know anyone there, but after the interview at a cafe, my American boss assured me I would have good accommodation and be looked after. So I said goodbye to my boyfriend and set off on the train.

It was all a new adventure. Settling in to my accommodation with an elderly couple, meeting new people on the job, operating equipment such as a teleprinter, electric typewriter, and a copying machine as big as a large dining table was just fantastic. A whole new world opened up for me.

It was an early start. At six thirty in the morning, the bus arrived, and I was on the job by seven. I finished at four thirty in the afternoon and arrived back home by five. The money piled up in my bank account. It helped that the office was smack in the middle of the plant project and to get into town at lunchtime was impossible, as there wasn't always a ride offered. The shops were closed by the time we arrived back in town in the afternoon, and once the project got going, we worked Saturday morning as well. There wasn't much to do in town; my life was made up of long working hours, church on Sunday, and nights writing long love letters. My boyfriend drove down once a month to visit me, borrowing his father's car.

I did make some good friends, and sometimes we met at the movies on Saturday night, or drove around the town in my friend's little Mini Minor car. After working and being away from home for a year, though, I thought it time to quit. I had only taken the job on my mother's persuasion. In those days, you listened to your parents. The experience of moving away from home and seeing other people and places was wonderful. By the time I was twenty-two years of age, I was married and living on the road in a caravan. Touring around Australia gave me a broader view of the world.

CHAPTER 21

❧❦❧

A Life Well Lived

The heavy rain is drumming on the aluminium roof in the entertainment area. My family is seated at the table. As I look around, I see my daughter, her three daughters, and a friend. It is her forty-second birthday, and I am in awe of the long journey to this point in her life—and her willingness to trust me enough to take those difficult steps that have brought her independence. I never knew her capabilities or her potential, but together we defeated all the naysayers, the critics, and the spiteful comments intended to bring us down.

Reaching for the stars is a daring project, but until we try, we will never know what we are made of or what miracles lie ahead. And yes, I do believe in miracles. I have seen too many not to believe. Life is made up of many different people. Think of how different each friend is, and the gifts that each one brings to us. People with disabilities are a part of that rich tapestry of life, and they have much to teach us.

To have hope when all around seems to lie in ashes requires a strength and endurance that is not granted to a special few; we all have it buried deep inside. For me, the secret to finding it was always in prayer and reading a special passage from a book that spoke to me at the time. Reading other people's wisdom is a gift; it takes us outside ourselves and shines a light in the darkness when we are at our lowest ebb.

To put one foot in front of the other even when we don't want to takes courage. To do it again and again builds layers within us, and confidence starts to grow. I have never been a particularly confident person. I have my doubts and fears just like anyone else—often more than others. But somehow my spirit drives me on, and I find myself being transformed again on another level that I didn't know was possible. To take someone with me on that journey has been a privilege and an honour. I am humbled by Lourdes' courage and tenacity. A lot of people only sip the bubbles off the top of the glass, others drain it to the dregs. I know we did.